# Better/Cheaper College
## An Entrepreneur's Guide to Rescuing the Undergraduate Education Industry

Vance H. Fried

*Larry
Thanks for SSB's
support
Vance*

Copyright 2010 by Vance. H. Fried
All rights reserved

Published by the Center for College Affordability and Productivity, LLC

978-0-615-40905-4

Printed in the United States of America
First Edition

*To My Parents*

# Acknowledgments

I owe thanks to many individuals over the last several years who have provided me with valuable assistance and insight in developing the ideas expressed in this book. During this time, I have been on the faculty of the Spears School of Business at Oklahoma State University, first in the Department of Management and now in the School of Entrepreneurship. Throughout this time, the School has been supportive of my research efforts. In particular, while working on this book I received encouragement and financial support from the School of Entrepreneurship and the Riata Center for Entrepreneurship.

A number of people offered helpful comments on the book manuscript at various stages, including Robert C. Andringa, Tom Brown, Michael Clifford, Brandon Dutcher, Ike Glass, Charles R. Greer, Jim Halligan, Henry Hansmann, Don Herrmann, Aaron Hill, Michael Hitt, Scott Johnson, Marilyn G. Kletke, George Leef, Bill McLean, Neal McCluskey, and John Mowen.

Chris Pryor provided overall editorial input in finalizing the book. At the Center for College Affordability and Productivity, Rich Vedder provided vital encouragement and input to this project. The manuscript was put to into its final form by CCAP research staff, including Andrew Gillen, Matthew Denhart, Jonathan Robe, Christopher Matgouranis, Jordan Shirkman, Michael Malesick, Christopher Denhart, as well as Kevin Cate for cover design and Bev Dunham for final formatting.

Finally, in recent years my wife and children have endured more than their fair share of discussion of this topic.

## Table of Contents

**Part I: Introduction –** *Better/Cheaper is Possible*

    Chapter 1 – An Entrepreneurial Perspective ................................ 1

**Part II: Barriers to Better/Cheaper –** *Why College are High Cost/ Mediocre Quality*

    Chapter 2 – Culture ........................................................................ 9

    Chapter 3 – Ownership ................................................................ 17

    Chapter 4 – Morals ...................................................................... 25

**Part III: Designing a Better/Cheaper College –** *A Step-by-Step Guide*

    Chapter 5 – Identify a Target Market .......................................... 33

    Chapter 6 – Define a Value Proposition ...................................... 41

    Chapter 7 – Pick the Right Activities to Perform ......................... 51

    Chapter 8 – Perform Activities the Right Way ............................ 65

    Chapter 9 – Develop an Organizational Physiology that Fits ....... 81

**Part IV: Conclusion –** *Making Better/Cheaper a Reality*

    Chapter 10 – Take Action ............................................................ 97

**Endnotes** .............................................................................................. 115

**Index** ................................................................................................... 123

**Appendices** ......................................................................................... 129

# Part I

# Introduction
## *Better/Cheaper is Possible*

**Chapter 1:**   **An Entrepreneurial Perspective**

# 1

# An Entrepreneurial Perspective

Several excellent books have been written about higher education in recent years, so why read this one? This book is different in that it takes an entrepreneurial perspective. Where other books see an industry with huge problems, this book sees an industry with huge opportunities. Where other books propose ways to tweak the existing higher education business model, this book proposes innovative business models to revolutionize the industry. Where other books look to the education establishment to lead change, this book looks to the entrepreneur to drive change. Where other books are aimed at slowing the rate of growth in tuition, this book advocates a radical reduction. The Better/Cheaper College of this book provides a better quality education than is available anywhere today at a cost of under $8,000. Combined with existing levels of state and private philanthropic support, Better/Cheaper College would often make a college education tuition free.

## Opportunity

Today's higher education industry presents great opportunities for entrepreneurs. It is an industry ripe for radical change—change that will benefit the successful entrepreneur and society as a whole.

- Today's colleges are charging historically high prices for a mediocre quality product. An entrepreneur with an innovative business model (the Better/Cheaper College) can offer higher quality at a lower price.
- Today's colleges are highly profitable businesses. A social entrepreneur willing to forgo high profits can use the Better/Cheaper College and cut price radically to make education more affordable.
- Today's higher education industry is highly fragmented. The biggest brands like Harvard are not interested in increasing market share at the undergraduate level.

- The old, inferior business model is deeply embedded throughout the industry. Most colleges have a culture that elevates the needs of its employees over its students. Decision-making is notoriously slow and politicized.
- While legally non-profits, in reality most colleges are owned by an employee collective of administrators and faculty. As employees, most members of the collective are comfortable working under the old model and reluctant to change. As owners, most would like to maintain high profits. In fact, many would lose their jobs under the Better/Cheaper College business model. As a result, most incumbents will be very slow to respond to aggressive competitors using the Better/Cheaper College.

This combination of a large market, superior business model, and slow-to-respond, incumbents makes the industry very attractive to an entrepreneur. From a societal standpoint, the success of entrepreneurs operating as Better/Cheaper Colleges will gradually remake the whole higher education industry both better and cheaper.

## High Price/Mediocre Quality

In recent years, several books have rightly pointed out the major quality and cost problems at today's colleges. Test results for recent college graduates reveal a level of knowledge and abilities in reading, writing, arithmetic and history that is shockingly low.[1] When a long-time president of Harvard University entitles his book about undergraduate education *Our Underachieving Colleges,* it is a good sign that we have major quality problems. But it's not just the 3Rs that suffer. There is also a major values crisis in higher education that has a perverse impact on students and society.[2]

At the same time, the price of college has skyrocketed. In 1970, $12,000 (in today's dollars) covered full-tuition for a year at Harvard. Today, $12,000 covers in-state tuition at Pennsylvania State University–Mont Alto (and that's only if you're from Pennsylvania and the state has chipped in an additional $6,000). Now that's for a small, regional commuter college. If you want Joe Paterno's Penn State, you'll need to cough up $17,000 if you're a Pennsylvania resident or $29,500 if you're not.

As you can see from Figure 1, average college tuition has tripled over the last thirty years, and that's after adjusting for inflation.

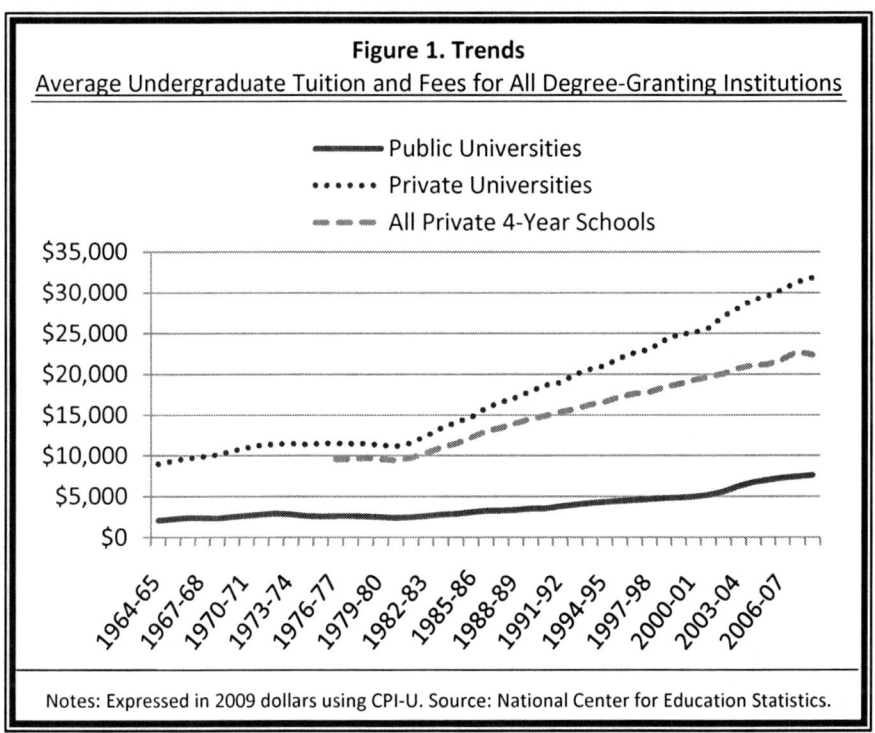

Figure 1. Trends
Average Undergraduate Tuition and Fees for All Degree-Granting Institutions

Notes: Expressed in 2009 dollars using CPI-U. Source: National Center for Education Statistics.

## The Better/Cheaper College

As a professor of entrepreneurship (and a parent of college students), I often wondered if a different business model could lower cost and raise quality. So a few years ago in *The $7,376 Ivies*, I looked at undergraduate education for traditional students as if I were exploring a new venture opportunity. Could I design a college that was better and cheaper?

I started by creating a business model for a hypothetical college and then determined its cost by developing a detailed pro forma income statement. My basic design premise was simple: maximize value to the student. Determine what package of benefits (primarily learning) and price is attractive to them. If an activity has a high cost but provides a substantial benefit, then do it; but do it as efficiently as possible. If an activity adds significant cost but only minor benefits, don't do it. I didn't cut any corners with my hypothetical college. A laptop is included in tuition, there is a residential college system like Harvard and Yale, faculty are high quality, the football stadium has a Jumbotron, etc.

I named my hypothetical school the College of Entrepreneurial Leadership & Society (CELS). CELS is for traditional undergraduate college students of moderately selective to highly selective academic standing who want to be actively involved in the college experience. CELS will offer a broad curriculum that provides students with a strong liberal education, appropriate technical skill for entry level jobs, potential to be general manager of an organization in their chosen profession early in their career, plus foundational skills and knowledge for life outside of work. The curriculum, operations and cost structure of CELS are described in detail in the Appendix of this book.

I think CELS would provide a package of benefits to its students that is much better than any existing college, including the "top" liberal arts colleges. Others may not share this view because they want to serve a different set of students needing a different mix of benefits. That is fine. The market for higher education is large with multiple segments. There are several possible versions of the Better/Cheaper College.

When I priced out CELS, the savings were striking. With 3,200 students, it would have a total operating cost (without room and board) of under $7,376 per student. Not surprisingly the Better/Cheaper Colleges cost is drastically below tuition at "top" liberal arts colleges ($25,000 to $62,000) but it is also substantially below the $12,000 cost (tuition plus state subsidy) of public regional commuter colleges.

## Today's Colleges

The negative feedback that I have received to *The $7,376 Ivies* isn't that my cost estimates weren't reasonable, or that CELS wouldn't provide a high quality institution, or that students wouldn't come. Rather, it's been "you could never get it done at a real college." The criticism is that while the Better/Cheaper College is clearly superior on paper, it requires a level of strategic innovation that administrators and faculty will not accept.

Why should they? If you look at colleges from the perspective of administrators and faculty, life is better than it has ever been. They have achieved de facto ownership of their colleges. The colleges they own have been able to drastically raise their prices without losing volume. As a result, profits are high with little need to retain capital in the business. Unfortunately, since the colleges they own are legally non-profits, they are not allowed to pay out all the profits directly to themselves as dividends. However, they are able to spend these profits on themselves and their personal academic agendas. Today is a golden era for most faculty and administrators.

You can see this in the high profit margins reported by successful for-profit colleges like the University of Phoenix but profits margins are even higher at non-profit colleges, both private and state owned. Of course, non-profits don't show all their profits on their books. Instead most are shown as expenses. Non-profit's reap their "profits" in the form of excess spending on some combination of research, graduate education, low demand majors, low faculty teaching loads, excess compensation and featherbedding. By using the term "profits" to describe this spending, I am not making a value judgment as to whether this spending is good for society. Rather, the point of the term that it is spending beyond what is necessary to provide a student with a high quality education. It is spending that provides no benefits to students.

As CELS demonstrates, providing a high-quality, undergraduate education in a residential setting costs about $8,000 per year per student.[3] The average private undergraduate college has net tuition revenues of $13,515 per student per year plus $7,292 per student per year in donations and endowment income.[4] So based on tuition revenues alone, the average private undergraduate school makes about $5,500 per student. When you add in donations and endowment income, profits jump to $12,800 per student. That's over a 60% net profit margin per student!!! The Better/Cheaper College will not be popular at most of today's colleges because it strives to eliminate the profits paid to the college's current de facto owners.

There certainly are major internal barriers to innovation within colleges today. Immediate industry-wide adoption of Better/Cheaper isn't going to happen. Rather, as the subtitle of the book suggests, the Better/Cheaper College will come from entrepreneurial action, not the established education bureaucracy. New Better/Cheaper

Colleges can be created that are free of the problems of existing colleges. An existing college can become Better/Cheaper today if it will truly decide to put the needs of students over their own profits. As Better/Cheaper Colleges emerge, the established members of the industry will have to change their ways or lose significant market share, and perhaps go out of business. The ultimate outcome of this creative destruction will be a massive benefit for students and society.

## Book Overview

The rest of the book is in three parts. Part 2 explains how colleges work today, focusing on the major internal barriers to implementation of the Better/Cheaper College at existing colleges. There are separate chapters on the three major barriers: Ivory Tower culture, employee collective ownership and morals incompatible with a liberal education.

Understanding these barriers is important. A new entrant needs to make sure their college avoids these three problems. An existing college wanting to convert to Better/Cheaper needs to understand the major internal barriers that have to be overcome. This part is entitled Barriers to Innovation because they are negatives for incumbents wanting to become Better/Cheaper. Alternatively, this part could be entitled Barriers to Response as they are positives for entrepreneurs because they limit the competitive response of incumbents.

Part 3 is a guide to designing a Better/Cheaper College. It goes through the steps in the general business model development process and provides several suggestions specific to the design of a Better/Cheaper College. Part 3 includes chapters on:

- ❖ Identify a target market
  - Vital because students, not faculty, are the primary workers in the production process
  - Ignore prestige-seeking students and their parents
  - Academic super-elitism is bad for undergraduate education
  - Many viable segments – one size doesn't fit all
- ❖ Define a value proposition
  - Match value proposition with target market
  - Challenge and support all students

- Bachelor's level needs mix of liberal, general technical and vocational education
- Viable approaches to liberal education – Natural Law, Church College, American Order

❖ Pick the right activities to perform (and not perform)
- Coherent curriculum with modular architecture
- Mass customization with personal attention
- No low-enrollment majors
- Manage and fund research separately (if at all)
- Student life is a waste for commuter segments

❖ Perform the activities the right way
- Use small classes only when pedagogically necessary
- Promote active learning
- Appropriate use of technology is cost/quality win/win
- Empty buildings are a waste of resources
- Permanent endowments are a waste of resources

❖ Develop an organizational physiology (structure, systems/processes, people and culture) consistent with the model
- Flatten structure – stress product/market over disciplinary grouping
- Manage large multi-college universities as confederations
- Manage colleges like a professional services firm
- Teaching undergraduates is nursing, not brain surgery
- Good people are mandatory
- Faculty jobs offer reasonable pay with significant non-financial rewards

Part 4 provides suggestions for various audiences interested in the immediate implementation of Better/Cheaper Colleges. It includes sections for:
- Small private colleges – do it now
- Large state research universities – create semi-autonomous Better/Cheaper Colleges
- For-profit colleges – Better/Cheaper may increase market share
- Faculty entrepreneurs – create faculty-owned companies to manage non-profit colleges
- State governments – break up your state college cartel and create private charter colleges to increase competition

- Large donors – don't put more money into the old model, instead start an industry revolution by supporting a Better/Cheaper pioneer

Action taken today can yield immediate benefits to those willing to act.

# Part II

# Barriers to Better/Cheaper
## *Why Colleges are High Cost/ Mediocre Quality*

Chapter 2:   Culture

Chapter 3:   Ownership

Chapter 4:   Morals

# 2

# Culture

Existing colleges face major internal barriers to implementing the Better/Cheaper College. Academia has a very strong organizational culture,[5] which is opposed to being Better/Cheaper. The Academic Ethic, or what outsiders call the Ivory Tower, is an industry-wide culture that both dominates and transcends today's colleges. "Learning for Learning's Sake" is the core value of the Ivory Tower. The Ivory Tower culture causes colleges to regularly behave in a manner that both drives cost up and pushes student benefits down. It is so embedded into the thinking of most faculty and administrators that they do not realize their actions often hurt, not help, students.

## Learning is a Means to a Better Life for the Student

As long-time Harvard President Derek Bok points out, the problems caused by the Ivory Tower culture are particularly acute at the undergraduate level.

> (Faculty) are preoccupied with the challenge of discovering and transmitting knowledge and ideas. To them, knowledge is not a means to other ends; it is an end in itself—indeed, the principal end of academic life. Most students, on the other hand, have different reason for acquiring a college education. They tend to look upon knowledge and ideas less as ends in themselves and more as means to accomplishing other goals, such as becoming better, more mature human beings or achieving success in their careers.[6]

Learning as a means to an end—a better life for the student—is not a new idea in higher education. It was the original purpose of American higher education. Higher education in America started with Harvard, founded as a Puritan college in 1636. The purpose of college in the Puritan view was elegantly stated by the poet John Milton in his treatise *Of Education*:

I call therefore for a complete and generous education, that which **fits a man to perform** justly, skillfully, and magnanimously, all the offices, both private and public, of peace and war. (emphasis added)[7]

This focus on learning as a means to an end also informed the creation of public schools in America. In 1818 Thomas Jefferson, James Madison, and other leading Virginians who served as the first commissioners for the University of Virginia met at the tavern in Rockfish Gap to found the university. In their official report, Jefferson wrote about the purposes of higher education:

To form the statesmen, legislators and judges, on whom public prosperity and individual happiness are so much to depend;

To expound the principles and structure of government, the laws which regulate the intercourse of nations, those formed municipally for our own government, and a sound spirit of legislation, which, banishing all arbitrary and unnecessary restraint on individual action, shall leave us free to do whatever does not violate the equal rights of another;

To harmonize and promote the interests of agriculture, manufactures and commerce, and by well informed views of political economy to give a free scope to the public industry;

To develop the reasoning faculties of our youth, enlarge their minds, cultivate their morals, and instill into them the precepts of virtue and order;

To enlighten them with mathematical and physical sciences, which advance the arts, and administer to the health, the subsistence, and comforts of human life;

And, generally, to form them to habits of reflection and correct action, rendering them examples of virtue to others, and of happiness within themselves.

These are the objects of that higher grade of education, the benefits and blessings of which the Legislature now propose to provide for the good and ornament of their country, the gratification and happiness of their fellow-citizens, of the parent especially, and his progeny, on which all his affections are concentrated.

The founding purpose of American higher education, whether public or private, was to provide students with learning so that they might lead a better life, both for their own benefit and that of society. While most students and society see learning as a means to an end, most colleges operate on a deeply held belief that learning is the end in itself. This belief in knowledge as the end, rather than a means to an end, is a central tenant of what is referred to by sociologists as the "Academic Ethic", and by most of the public as the "Ivory Tower." The Ivory Tower mentality consistently results in a cost/benefit lose/lose for students.

## Ivory Tower and Curriculum

To illustrate this lose/lose outcome, let's take a look at undergraduate curriculum. The curriculum (from the Latin for "race course") is the primary set of activities that students perform to earn their educations. Paying faculty to teach its curriculum is every college's biggest expense item. So, the design of the curriculum should be really important to both student and college.

Undergraduate curriculum is generally broken down into three parts: general education, a major, and electives. General education is a rather vague concept. To quote the Higher Learning Commission, one of the major accrediting groups in the U.S.:

> Understanding and appreciating diverse cultures, mastering multiple modes of inquiry, effectively analyzing and communicating information, and recognizing the importance of creativity and values to the human spirit not only allow people to live richer lives but also are a foundation for most careers and for the informed exercise of local, national, and international citizenship.
>
> Throughout its history, the Commission has believed that quality undergraduate higher education involves breadth as well as depth of study. As understood by the Commission, general education is intended to impart common knowledge and intellectual concepts to students and to develop in them the skills and attitudes that an organization's faculty believe. From an organization's general education, a student acquires a breadth of knowledge in the areas and proficiency in the skills that the organization defines as being the hallmark of being college educated. Moreover, effective general education helps students gain competence in the exercise of

independent intellectual inquiry and also stimulates their examination and understanding of personal, social and civic values.

Now this may sound good in principal, but reality at most colleges is very different. Ross Douthat, *New York Times* columnist and 2001 Harvard grad wrote an *Atlantic Monthly* article[8] (and later a book[9]) in which he vented about his college education. He was frustrated by general education classes like "Women Writers in Imperial China: How to Escape from the Feminine Voice" and "Dinosaurs and their Relatives." In his words, "I set out with the intention of picking a comprehensive roster of classes that would lead...in directions at once interesting and essential, providing perspectives that were unavailable in my concentration."

How successful was he? He cites only *one* course that was taught by an "enthusiastic professor" that "proved to be spectacular." In other classes he encountered disengaged professors or teaching assistants, as well as tepid content.

Michael Clifford, the catalyst behind the conversion of Grand Canyon University from near bankrupt non-profit to NYSE growth company, is also outspoken on the problems of general education.[10]

In my work with many different colleges, I've read a lot of college catalogues. As you peruse them, you'll come across some pretty unusual courses. The candidates for most unusual course are numerous, but as a former professional musician, here are couple of my personal favorites.

- *Girl Culture*. This Duke class covers all-female bands and other essentials of female culture like the Powerpuff Girls cartoon, teenage fairies and witches, dolls, dress-up, makeovers and slumber parties.
- *Music of the Grateful Dead*. You can take a whole course in Jerry Garcia at the University of California-Santa Cruz. What could be a better use of time and tuition?

Why do these ridiculous and irrelevant classes exist, and why do students have to take general education courses that do not in the least prepare them for their future vocations? I have repeatedly posed this question to faculty, accreditors, DOE representatives, school presidents, and others involved in education. All respond with the same basic answer, almost as if it has been hard-wired into their brains: the purpose of general education is to teach students critical thinking skills. If this were true, it would be wonderful. However, students exposed to these classes do not exhibit any improved critical thinking skills.

I have to say, after spending countless hours with the freshmen and sophomores subjected to these marginally useful classes, their thinking skills are rapidly being dulled rather than sharpened. What *is* critical thinking anyway? Is it anything more than good old common sense?

Douthat and Clifford aren't the only critics. General education at most colleges is roundly and regularly criticized by pundits. In fact, just about everybody is critical of general education curriculum, except for the faculty that design it (and some of them aren't too thrilled). So why does a curriculum that is supposed to teach critical thinking skills result in a curriculum that reflects a total lack of common sense?

Let's think from a professor's viewpoint. "Since the purpose of college is learning for the joy of learning, what could be better and more joyful for the student than learning about what I'm interested in? Since I'm interested in Deadheads and Powerpuff Girls, they certainly have a place in General Education." (Coincidentally this also results in a class that is easier for the professor to teach since all she has do is talk about her niche interests).

Now let's look from the perspective of the various disciplinary departments. In the Ivory Tower, Knowledge is god. Each department wants their specific god (Disciplinary Knowledge) to be Zeus in the college's Pantheon. The department fervently believes that it is in the student's best interest to worship the best god. Of course, it also leads to the department getting more and better paid priests and a nicer temple. Sadly, the design of the general education curriculum is driven by internal politics between various disciplinary departments who compete to place their discipline's Knowledge front and center.

Harry R. Lewis, former Dean of Harvard College (the undergraduate part of Harvard) describes the result

> Typically students are required to distribute their course selections across odd categories such as "Quantitative Reasoning" and "Social Analysis" in Harvard's current curriculum. The more those categories result from academic

border skirmishes rather than an overarching vision, the more likely they are to be ugly compromises, forged out of what Harvard students accurately call "a tangled web of earnest, academic motivations." The professors doing the design may be content with defending their own turf. But the students, who during their journey through the college curriculum have to visit the homelands of many professors, wonder at the end of the trip what it was all about.[11]

The Ivory Tower also looks down its nose at "mere" skills training. Derek Bok explains:

> The past few decades have seen advances in analyzing and teaching new competencies that were previously thought to be a skill one either was born with or had to learn for oneself—skills such as facility in interpersonal relations, or the ability to communicate effectively across cultural boundaries, or techniques of mediation, negotiation, and leadership. As more becomes known about such competencies, students express interest in mastering them because of their value in helping to achieve a variety of desired ends—not only advancement in one's career but also success in community activities, in marriage, and even in such mundane tasks as bargaining over the price of a new car. Arts and Science professors, however, tend to be wary of these emerging subjects and often balk at including them in the curriculum. To many scholars, the newer competencies lack intellectual depth and call for a kind of cookbook training unsuitable for a proper university.[12]

## Ivory Tower and College Organization

The impact of the Ivory Tower Culture on colleges goes far beyond the curriculum. It includes the concepts of individual faculty autonomy, tenure, departments organized by academic disciplines, specialization, superiority of research over teaching, and individual faculty being more devoted to their discipline (or subdiscipline) than their college.[13] The Ivory Tower became dominate in America by the early 20th century. James Pierson, formerly a political science professor at the University of Pennsylvania and now senior fellow at the Manhattan Institute, explains:

> The institutional model was the University of Berlin, established in 1810 by Wilhelm von Humboldt, Prussian minister

of education, under the influence of the idealist philosophers Fichte, Kant, and Hegel, who asserted that the task of the scholar was to search for the truth in science, philosophy, and morals unimpeded by political or religious authorities. The University of Berlin, the original research university, was based on the idea that truth is not something known and passed on, but the subject of persistent inquiry and continuous revision. It incorporated the practice of faculty autonomy in the selection of subjects for research and course work, and conceived of students as junior partners in the research enterprise, that is, as professors in training. This new institution thus recast the purpose of the university away from theology, tradition, and vocations and in the direction of science and secular studies. It discarded as well the practice of looking to ancient writers for moral lessons and political guidance. The new university thus placed the faculty rather than students, religious bodies, or public officials at the center of the enterprise, for it was the faculty that in the end would decide what was studied and taught. ...

The faculty, as the new priesthood of the research enterprise would shortly claim authority to decide all matters dealing with curriculum, new faculty appointments, and promotions. The modern doctrine of academic freedom, which gives professors wide latitude to teach and conduct research as they wish, also followed in due course as a consequence of these premises. Much as Oliver Wendell Holmes said that the law is what judges say it is, the reformed university would henceforth be whatever the faculty decides. [14]

While the Ivory Tower may have benefited scientific research, it has had a negative impact on education. It has made today's colleges dysfunctional organizations. Boston College professor Alan Wolfe describes today colleges as having "a feudal culture, a system based on the principle of protecting the autonomy of independent guilds..." Wolfe points out that this feudal culture has a negative effect on college productivity.

> Operating in a feudal organizational system, academics are quick to adopt a feudal code of conduct. Charles Anderson describes it succinctly: "If each leaves the other alone, then we can all do as we please." Every college, every department,

every individual, is a fiefdom. This is not, despite what some critics say, a "laissez faire" system. In that kind of system individuals (or organizations) are concerned with what others do, obsessively so; they know that if a competitor offers a better, cheaper product than they do, they may go under. The operating rules of the university resemble a Mafia "honor" code more than a regime of laissez faire: it's best not to inquire too deeply into anyone else's activities. If I ask the purpose of what you are doing, you will ask the same of me, and before long the rational for the enterprise will begin to crumble.[15]

It is really hard for people outside of education to understand the Ivory Tower mindset. I've been on a big research university faculty (albeit in a professional school) for 23 years, and I still don't get it. But I can attest that it is widely held among faculty and administrators (who, after all, used to be faculty), and it is an extremely strong force in college decision-making. Unfortunately, it often leads to decisions that are not in the best interests of students. It is a huge barrier to the Better/Cheaper College. Education must be grounded in the proposition that learning is primarily a means to an end, not the end in itself. Education should focus on the student, not the Ivory Tower and the interests of faculty and administrators. Colleges today are focused on serving the Ivory Tower, not their students.

# 3

# Ownership

Another major barrier to strategic innovation is the ownership structure of most higher education institutions. Most are legally organized as non-profits, many of whom are state-owned institutions; but in practice, colleges are owned by a collective of administrators and faculty devoted to the Ivory Tower. Colleges are managed by this collective for the benefit of the collective and the Ivory Tower.

## "Profitable" Non-Profits

The cheaper part of Better/Cheaper runs counter to the way that colleges currently price. Colleges take a high price/high profit margin approach. Over the last 30 years, this strategy has worked very well. Most colleges have extremely high profit margins. They like having high profit margins. They show no desire to reduce their profit margins. In fact, they constantly are trying to push their margins up.

Now improving profit margins is a common goal of a for-profit firm. The for-profit firm does this as means to increase profits for its investor/owners. So who are the owners of a college? Legally ownership confers two formal rights: the right to control operations of the firm and the right to appropriate the firm's profits.[16] Formally, most colleges are organized as non-profits. The right to control is vested in a board of trustees, and it is illegal to appropriate its profits to anyone. In reality, however, the situation is very different. Control of operations rests in an administrator/faculty collective, and profits are paid out to this collective in the form of unnecessary expenditures.

In the rest of this book, I will refer to the true owners of the college as the "Ivory Tower Collective (ITC)," and the excess spending as "ITC profits." By using the phrase ITC profits, I am not making a value judgment as to whether this excess spending is good for society; rather, the point of the term is that this is spending by the college that is not necessary to provide a student a high-quality education. For example, let's assume that the market position of the college is such that it can charge a net tuition of about $20,000. The real cost of providing this education is $8,000. The college prices at $20,000 and makes $12,000 in ITC profits that are spent on some combination of research, graduate education, low demand majors, excess compensation, and featherbedding.

The primary members of the ITC are the college's administrators and faculty. I use the term Ivory Tower Collective rather than Administrator/Faculty Collective because most of the Collective's members are true believers in the Ivory Tower and are interested in its advancement.

In the ITC, no one person is truly in charge and no one specifically owns the ITC profits. True, the president has the most decision-making authority, but this is highly limited by the other members of the ITC.[17] In order to get and maintain the job of CEO, the president must curry favor with the ITC. The president can distribute profits among various members of the ITC but is limited in the amount of profit that can be distributed to any one member of the ITC ($1 million plus presidential salaries[18] not withstanding).

In the ITC-owned college, decisions are made politically by the members of the ITC and profits are distributed indirectly through these decisions. Each member competes politically; first, for their own economic interests (higher salary, less work, more resources to support their research, etc.) and second for the programs of their department. To the extent behavior is not economically driven, the primary motive is the advancement of the member's personal research agenda, the academic discipline, and the prestige of the overall ITC.

Luckily, all members of the ITC are not as self-serving as this analysis presents. While the ITC overall does not care much about undergraduate education, many individual faculty do care, and many are very good at instruction. Unfortunately, many don't care. The result is an uncoordinated education of spotty quality.

While faculty through their individual efforts can improve benefits to students, they can do nothing about reducing costs. There is no point for any member of the ITC to forego ITC profits to reduce costs to students. It just won't happen. Any profits not captured by one member of the ITC will simply be captured by another.

Also, even student-oriented members of the ITC may not see ITC profits as a bad thing. Since the Ivory Tower is a good thing, then ITC profits are a good thing. Spending can never be excessive if it furthers the Ivory Tower. If the purpose of the Ivory Tower is Learning for Learning's sake, what better way to spend money than on Learning?

Like any organization, the rationality of decisions made by a college is limited by the knowledge limits of man. But beyond that, colleges are even less rational because they utilize a collective decision-making process. Because the interests of the various members of the ITC making the decision are diverse, the ultimate decisions are often irrational given the knowledge possessed.[19]

To the extent decisions are made rationally, the financial objective of the non-profit college is to maximize ITC profits by maximizing revenues. Exclusive private colleges emphasize maximizing revenues per student so as to maximize ITC profits per collective member.[20] On the other hand, public colleges are often more concerned with maximizing total revenues so as to maximize total ITC profits.

In addition to revenues from students, non-profit colleges also receive revenues from donations. State-owned colleges also receive large subsidies from the state taxpayer. Colleges seek to maximize revenues from these other sources as well. Colleges aggressively seek donor money to add buildings and programs but not to reduce tuition revenues. Similarly, when a state budget crisis necessitates lowering the state subsidy, colleges are quick to raise tuition to make up for the revenue loss, but when the state subsidy goes back up, tuition is never reduced accordingly.

It is understandable that the ITC likes high ITC profits. It is the recipient of the profits. The real question is why the institutions themselves seek high ITC profits. After all, they are legally organized as non-profits to operate for the benefit of their students, not the ITC. How did we get to our current position of high prices for students and high profits for the ITC?

## Bowen's Law

Thirty years ago, Howard R. Bowen, an economist and president of three different colleges, proposed what are known in education circles as Bowen's Laws. They can be summarized as "colleges raise all the money they can, and spend all the money they can raise." Bowen presented his laws as follows.

1. The dominant goals of institutions are educational excellence, prestige, and influence.

    The "excellence" or "quality" of institutions are commonly judged by such criteria as faculty-student ratios, faculty salaries, number of Ph.D.s on the faculty, number of books in the library, range of facilities and equipment, and academic qualifications of students. These criteria are resource inputs most of which cost money, not outcomes flowing from the educational process. The true outcomes in the form of learning and personal development of students are on the whole unexamined and only vaguely discerned.

2. In the quest of excellence, prestige, and influence, there is virtually no limit to the amount of money an institution could spend for seemingly fruitful educational ends.

    Whatever level of expenditure is attained is seldom considered enough. Institutions tend, therefore, to spend up to the very limit of their means. As a result, the financial problems of rich institutions are about as severe as those of all but the most impoverished institutions. This is especially so because whatever expenditures are once admitted into the budget become long-term commitments from which it is difficult ever to withdraw.

3. Each institution raises all the money it can.

    No college or university ever admits to having enough money and all try to increase their resources without limit.

4. Each institution spends all it raises.

    Many institutions, however, accumulate reserves and endowments. These "savings" are derived primarily from gifts designated for endowment and not from voluntary allocations of current income. In most institutions, the accumulations are of negligible amount. The few institutions that become very affluent, however, are able to save substantial amounts and accumulate significant endowments.

5. The cumulative effect of the preceding four laws is toward ever-increasing expenditure.

    The incentives inherent in the goals of excellence, prestige, and influence are not counteracted within the higher educational system by incentives leading to parsimony or efficiency. **The question of what *ought* higher education to cost—what is the minimal amount needed to provide services of acceptable quality—does not enter the process** except as it is imposed from the outside. The higher educational system itself provides no guidance of a kind that weighs costs and benefits in terms of the public interest. The duty of setting limits thus falls, by default, upon those who provide the money, mostly legislators and students and their families (emphasis added).[21]

Bowen proposed his Laws back in 1980. The cost explosion of the last 30 years has proven Bowen right to the extreme.[22] While chasing prestige has long been a goal of a few schools, it really wasn't that dominant in the mindset of most schools. That changed with the rise of the college ratings, particularly the annual rankings published by *U.S. News and World Report*. For the last three decades, the mantra of most college presidents and boards has been to move up in the ratings. However, the ratings don't have anything to do with how well a college educates its students; instead, they focus on how much money it can spend. As Kevin Carey concluded in his analysis of the various components of the *U.S. News* ratings, "the influential rankings have led colleges and universities to focus their energies on becoming wealthier, more famous, and more exclusive, often at the expense of what matters most—educating their students well."[23] Given this focus, it is no wonder that costs have soared.

Robert E. Martin, an economics professor with substantial experience as a faculty member at both the large state research university and the small liberal arts college, recently expanded on Bowen's Laws:

> Reputations confer prestige, wealth, and a more stable and less risky income; so, it is no surprise that higher education institutions seek a reputation for excellence. Controversies always suggest that something is wrong—and that can only weaken reputation. Therefore, maximizing academic reputation means avoiding controversies, and avoiding controversies means avoiding reform. Since existing resources cannot be moved, the only way the university can finance new program demands is through increases in

external revenues—state support, tuition, donor gifts, or federal funds.

The desire for funding through additional revenues (rather than using revenues more efficiently by reallocating costs) does not mean that spending is completely out of control. It is capped by revenues. A university or college avoids spending more than its revenues.

But administrators have an incentive to spend every dollar that is available. They cannot spend more without appearing incompetent, but spending less would forgo the opportunity to make some members of their constituencies happier. Whatever is available is spent.

Administrators tend to allocate the increases in revenue across all programs, rather than concentrate them on a few (as business would be likely to do). By choosing the goal of elevating all programs, administrators avoid controversy about who will benefit. Indeed, administrators often attempt to make their university "one of the top 20 research universities in the country." Yet trying to raise all programs at the same time wastes resources and reduces the probability of actual improvement.

Revenues are the lid on expenditures during each period. Since existing resources are frozen in place, the resources required for the new initiatives that arise each year can only come from new revenues. Some of these new initiatives will be driven by competition; most will be the pet projects of faculty, administrators, or board members. In business, new initiatives are chosen on the basis of their expected return. In higher education, priorities are determined by internal politics.

Because all the revenues are spent each year, costs typically increase as a result of these initiatives. If money is given to faculty to start a new program, for example, that additional money will be expected in the next academic year as well—the faculty member is unlikely to go back to the previous salary. Thus, when revenues rise, costs rise to fill the gap between the last period's expenditures and the new revenues. This argument was originally presented in 1980 by H.R. Bowen.

Indeed, as the Bowen hypothesis suggests, higher education finance is a black hole that cannot be filled. The relationship between revenues and subsequent costs has a dynamic feedback effect. Higher education responds to higher costs by raising tuition and fees or initiating fund-raising campaigns. But because costs in higher education are capped only by total revenues, there is no incentive to minimize costs. The costs go up in tandem with revenues. The next year, the cycle begins again because the higher costs mean that the new programs must be financed by additional revenues. There is thus a never-ending spiral effect between revenues and cost.

As revenues increase, faculty, administrators, and board members extract more surplus from the cash flows in the form of higher costs and then use those higher costs as justification for more revenue. *Imagine the consumer's response if for-profit firms argued they had to raise prices because the surplus that they extracted during the last period (i.e., profit) increased.* [24]

## Eliminate ITC Profits

The result of all of this is that colleges constantly strive to increase profits.[25] They then pay these profits to the insiders at the expense of students and society. It is unlikely that most trustees realize what is happening. Many probably have a general idea but do not understand the magnitude. They do not have a clear picture of what costs really should be. The problem isn't just at the board level. In fact, few insiders (presidents included) have a good picture of what the costs should be. This needs to change, but understanding costs isn't enough.

A college has to change who gets its profits. Rather than the ITC, why not give the profits to your students in the form of lower tuition? Completely reverse the traditional college view on the relationship between revenue and cost. Eliminate accounting profits by reducing revenue, not increasing expenses. Determine what level of spending is necessary, and reduce revenues to this level. If a college is truly a non-profit, why should it have profits at the expense of its purpose?

# 4

# Morals

Why does a non-profit college seek to maximize insider profits at the expense of students and society? To many outsiders this behavior appears immoral. However, it is not immoral behavior in the eyes of most colleges. Other than their fervent devotion to the Ivory Tower, most colleges today are amoral organizations (some argue immoral).

To an amoral college, there is nothing wrong about being a highly profitable non-profit. There is nothing wrong with advancing the best interests of the ITC at the expense of those whom you purport to serve. The amorality of most colleges is a major barrier to reducing the cost of college. On top of that, it is a major barrier to providing a major benefit of college—a liberal education.

## Liberal Education

As discussed in Chapter 2, learning as a mean to an end—a better life for the student—was the original purpose of American higher education. Liberal education is a vital component of Milton's "complete and generous education that which fits a man to perform justly, skillfully, and magnanimously, all the offices, both private and public, of peace and war."[26]

Leland Ryken, a professor at Wheaton College (IL), explains further:

> The heart of Milton's definition is that a complete education is one that frees a person to perform "all the offices, both private and public." A liberal education is comprehensive. It prepares a person to do well all that he or she may be called to do in life.
>
> Learning a certain amount of information will not by itself constitute a liberal education. Such **knowledge becomes worthwhile only as it is instrumental in forming a qualified person**. The effects of a good education,

according to Milton, are twofold: **Education influences people in their personal lives, and it makes them productive members of society.** (emphasis added)

Education in our day often focuses on a single public role, that of job or vocation, which is increasingly defined in economic terms only. Milton's phrase "public offices" covers much more than that, however. It includes being a good church member and a positive contributor to the community.

And what are the "private offices" that Milton mentioned? They included being a good friend, roommate, spouse, or parent; and they include the most personal world of all—the inner world of the mind and imagination.[27]

Most people agree with Milton that a person's education should include a liberal education component. By liberal education, I'm referring to the modern versions of classical liberal education—an education for "libertas"—living as free citizens. This is far different from the current concept of a liberal arts education.

The culture of most modern colleges makes providing a liberal education impossible. To provide a liberal education requires that a college has moral values consistent with a liberal education. Many argue that the problem is that colleges are amoral institutions. They do not adhere to a clear and objective standard of moral values, so it is impossible for them to provide a liberal education. Others view the modern college as the Politically Correct University that espouses values that are diametrically opposed to liberal education because they are opposed to the concept of a free society. Either way, most colleges do not have appropriate moral values to provide a liberal education.

## Loose Graduates

There are serious ramifications to the failure of liberal education. Any time there is a business scandal, MBA programs are roundly criticized for the moral faults of their graduates. While MBA programs are not free from fault, the problem is more fundamental and widespread; as Rakesh Khurana, a professor at the Harvard Business School, describes:

Lacking either the religious framework invoked by the founders of the modern university and the university-based business school, or shared agreement about basic societal values, we have no meaningful language for civic discourse about the ultimate purpose of our secular institutions. Thus we have been left only with empty rhetoric about "excellence" or "leadership" with which to discuss the educational mission of the university. As a result, our universities are now apt to turn out what the late Robert Nisbet called "loose individuals." The loose individual Nisbet described is someone who does not feel constrained by norms arising from social values such as fairness or equity, or by allegiance to social institutions such as nations, firms, or even jobs. Such individuals lack any sense of "moral responsibility," often playing "fast and loose with the other individuals in relationships of trust and responsibility." Their relationships with those who are not their intimates are anchored only in utilitarian self-interest. Loose individuals thrive in amoral environments in which ideas such as duty and reciprocity seem alien or are ridiculed as old-fashioned and naïve. They respond only to the invisible hand, reflexively following market signals as though they were road signs indicating the appropriate direction for their actions.[28]

These loose individuals are not limited to the business world. They are in all sectors. Higher education today turns out many bright, ambitious, and loose individuals. They are destructive of society and, ultimately, of themselves.

But the problem goes well beyond the loose individual that today's colleges sometimes produce. Many, hopefully most, students come to college with the desire to be grounded individuals. They come to higher education seeking meaning beyond animalistic self-interest. They want an education that will prepare them for a whole life. While they are interested in a technical education that will teach them to do things excellently, they also want a liberal education that will address what things they should do excellently.

Students are not getting a liberal education at most colleges today. This has had a profound impact on both student and society. As Hoover Institution fellow and former Harvard and George Mason professor, Peter Berkowitz writes, "University education can cause lasting harm. The mental habits that students form and the ideas they absorb in college consolidate the framework through which as adults they interpret experience, and judge matters to be true or false, fair or inequitable, honorable or dishonorable. A university that fails to teach students sound mental habits and to acquaint them with enduring ideas handicaps its graduates for both public and private life."[29]

## Loose Institutions

Many argue that the reason for poor liberal education is that most colleges today are amoral. The title of Harry Lewis's book about his experiences as dean of Harvard College—*Excellence Without a Soul*—says a lot. Lewis concludes the book by saying:

> Harvard strives to be the best at many things, and it often succeeds. But Harvard has protected its reputation for excellence at the expense of a larger purpose. Harvard is no longer a city upon a hill but merely a brand name.[30]

This desire for academic excellence without any underlying purpose is descriptive of research universities in general, as well as most "national" liberal arts college. Then, as one moves down the academic pecking order, just substitute "mediocrity" for "excellence" and the description still holds.

This lack of institutional moral grounding renders impotent the founding purposes of education in the United States. Education institutions were founded to further religion, morality, and knowledge. In 1645, an act of the Massachusetts General Court granted a charter to the free school at Roxbury to provide education "as a means for the fitting of instruments for public service in church and commonwealth." Subsequently, Harvard's Charter of 1650 states the purpose of the institution as providing an education "to the English and Indian youth of this Country in knowledge and godliness."

The Puritans followed Harvard with Yale. While not founded directly by the Puritans, almost all private colleges in America until the 20th century were founded as Christian institutions under the Puritan liberal education model. Public education was founded with the same injunction. In 1787 the Continental Congress in the Northwest Ordinance set aside 1/36 of the land in the Northwest Territory (ultimately the states of Michigan, Ohio, Illinois, Indiana, Wisconsin, and a portion of Minnesota) "for the maintenance of public schools." The Ordinance declares that "Religion, morality, and knowledge being necessary to good government and the happiness of mankind, schools and the means of education shall ever be encouraged."[31]

American education was based on the propagation of religion, morality, and knowledge. This trinity wasn't just for private colleges, but also state universities. For example, mandatory chapel was the norm at state universities in 1890.

As Russell K. Nieli writes in *From Christian Gentlemen to Bewildered Seeker: The Transformation of Higher Education in America*,

> During the long period when education was dominated by Protestant clergymen and other dedicated Reformation Christians, the educational system had a clear purpose, focus, and coherence. There was one simple and overriding goal: the production of morally earnest Christian gentlemen, well versed in liberal learning and in the classics of Greco-Roman and biblical high culture, who would be able to assume leadership positions in American society, especially as clergymen, businessmen, lawyers, and elected officials. Not only the curriculum but the overall college experience in the age of ascendant Protestantism was marked by an overriding unity and a sense of collective purpose at once instructive and morally elevating. The culmination of this enterprise was the senior year course on moral philosophy, often taught by the college's clergyman president, which explained to the students their ultimate moral obligations to God, their families, their nation, and their church.
>
> The typical college curriculum in the eighteenth and early nineteenth centuries consisted of something very close to the medieval *trivium* (grammar, rhetoric, and logic) and *quadrivium* (arithmetic, astronomy, geometry, music), with the emphasis being on classical language learning (Latin and Greek) and mathematical knowledge. Besides the Bible, students would be expected to read many of the best of ancient Greek writers, including the tragedians, Plato, Aristotle, Xenophon, and Plutarch, as well as the best of the Latin authors, especially Cicero, Virgil, Livy, Seneca, and Marcus Aurelius. Instruction was generally uniform—everyone took the same prescribed course of study over a four-year period, with few if any "electives." The instructors, a large portion of whom were ordained clergymen, were expected to be "generalists" who could be called upon when necessary to teach a variety of courses. There were no

"research professors" or those not concentrated on the instruction of the young. College professors and tutors were also expected to set a good example in terms of moral rectitude and good Christian living for the students under their charge.[32]

Soon after the end of the Civil War, morally grounded education began a long decline with sporadic periods of renewal. Several factors, many tied with the overall decline of religion and moral philosophy in higher education, were involved.[33]

1. Student complaints about the curriculum being overlying intellectual, spiritually dry, and boring
2. Criticisms of the curriculum as high-church elitist
3. Increased need for technical education as America industrialized
4. Copying the German Research University model focused on creation of new knowledge rather than transmission of established knowledge
5. Reformed Protestantism's (Puritans, Congregationalists, and Presbyterians) desire for a unified American culture with it as the unofficial establishment church
6. Liberal Protestants taking control of elite private and public colleges and excluding more orthodox Protestants, Catholics, and others who did not subscribe to Liberal Protestantism
7. Rise of pure naturalism and positivism as the dominant philosophy of science
8. Rise of pragmatism as an absolute—promoting a "society in which everyone enjoyed fairness, worried only about solving immediate problems by generally agreed means, and got along happily—like a gigantic but carefully managed school recess"[34]
9. The emergence of post-modernism
10. The decline of mainline Protestant denominations
11. Counter-culture of 1960s
12. Abdication of control of curriculum and student life by many colleges to student pressure groups in the late 1960s

The net result was that by 1970 when I started college, the concept of a morally grounded education had all but disappeared, except at some traditional Protestant and Catholic colleges.

## Illiberal Education

Others argue that the problem isn't that colleges today are amoral. Rather, it is that most colleges have a belief system that is incompatible with a liberal education. In *Illiberal Education*, Dinesh D'Souza, now president of The King's College, writes:

> Each fall some 13 million students, 2.5 million of them minorities, enroll in American colleges. Most of these students are living away from home for the first time. Yet their apprehension is mixed with excitement and anticipation. At the university, they hope to shape themselves as whole human beings, both intellectually and morally. Brimming with idealism, they wish to prepare themselves for full and independent lives in the workplace, at home, and as citizens who are shared rulers of a democratic society. In short, what they seek is liberal education.
>
> By the time these students graduate, very few colleges have met their need for all-round development. Instead, by precept and example, universities have taught them that "all rules are unjust" and "all preferences are principled"; that justice is simply the will of the stronger party; that standards and values are arbitrary, and the ideal of the educated person is largely a figment of bourgeois white male ideology, which should be cast aside; that individual rights are a red flag signaling social privilege and should be subordinated to the claims of group interest; that all knowledge can be reduced to politics and should be pursued not for its own sake but for the political end of power; that convenient myths and benign lies can substitute for truth; that double standards are acceptable as long as they are enforced to the benefit of minority victims; that debates are best conducted not by rational and civil exchange of ideas, but by accusation, intimidation, and official prosecution; that the university stands for nothing in particular and has no claim to be exempt from outside pressures; and that the multiracial society cannot be based on fair rules that apply to every person, but must

rather be constructed through a forced rationing of power among separatist racial groups. In short, instead of liberal education, what American students are getting is its diametrical opposite, an education in closed-mindedness and intolerance, which is to say, illiberal education.[35]

While many may disagree with several of the allegations D'Souza makes in his second paragraph, few will contest what he said in the first paragraph or in the first sentence of the second. Most undergraduate students do expect a college education to include a liberal education. Few colleges deliver. Whether the problem is the Amoral University or the Politically Correct University (or perhaps some of both), most colleges today do not deliver a liberal education.

While the specifics of a college's moral values may vary from college to college (more about this in Chapter 6), it must have some. Otherwise, a college is a loose organization turning out loose individuals. It cannot provide a liberal education because it has no beliefs upon which to ground that education.

# Part III

# Designing a Better/Cheaper College
## *A Step-by-Step Guide*

Chapter 5:   Identify a Target Market

Chapter 6:   Define a Value Proposition

Chapter 7:   Pick the Right Activities to Perform

Chapter 8:   Perform Activities the Right Way

Chapter 9:   Develop an Organizational Physiology that Fits

# 5

# Identify a Target Market

The barriers to reducing cost and improving quality are high but not insurmountable. High quality at a reasonable price is achievable if a college adopts a new type of business model—the Better/Cheaper College. In this part of the book, I'll go through the basic steps in designing any business model and provide several specific suggestions on how to design a Better/Cheaper College.

The first step in designing a business model is identifying your target market. Private colleges have high sales and marketing expenses (euphemistically referred to as "admissions"). Properly identifying your target market can reduce these costs by making your efforts more efficient. But target market selection goes far beyond marketing. It is fundamental to designing a good business model. A good business model for one target market is often a bad business model for another.

## Segmenting the Market[36]

Higher education is a highly fragmented industry with over 4,338 institutions.[37] These institutions provide a wide variety of educational programs to the market. The existence of different segments with different student needs provides numerous opportunities to deliver different products using different business models.

Defining a clear market segment is particularly important for a college because the nature of education is very different from most goods.[38] The consumer (student) is the major raw material in the production process, so the quality of the output (graduating student) is heavily influenced by the quality of the input (matriculating student). Further, the student is the most important laborer in the process (more so than faculty). So unlike most goods, the amount of value created in the production process is driven largely by the efforts of the consumer (student).

In addition, education often is an associative good.[39] Unlike many goods for which value is defined by individual consumption, college is in part valued by the nature of the commonly shared experience with other consumers. A related issue is the post-consumption value of the degree. The degree is a credential whose value is influenced by who else holds the degree. In addition, the degree also gives the holder access to the informal network of the college in the form of alumni and employers who are tied to the college.

The higher education industry can be segmented in numerous ways. Common segmentations are by geographic location, degree level, subject matter, student age, full-time or part-time attendance, residential or commuter living, extent and nature of values education, online or place-based delivery, and academic selectivity of students.

A Better/Cheaper College can be designed to serve any of these segments or their various combinations. However, it is fundamental to the Better/Cheaper College to segment by the student's, or perhaps more often their parents', view on the relationship between price and quality. The three basic views are prestige-oriented (exclusivity at a high price), value-oriented (high quality at a reasonable price) and price-oriented (the cheapest thing that works). The Better/Cheaper College is for the value-oriented. This is the largest sector of the college market and is currently dominated by the state research universities.

## College Isn't Just for the Academic Super-Elite

The level of academic selectivity of the "top" colleges and universities is vastly higher than can be justified for educational reasons. From the data they report, their average entering student has an IQ[40] in the top 1%. There are millions of people who are smart enough to do extremely well academically in college that aren't up to the level of hyperselectivity that these prestige schools desire. This is even more true when you move from academic success to career success. Take George Washington, Franklin Roosevelt, Harry Truman, Dwight Eisenhower, John F. Kennedy, Lyndon Johnson, or Ronald Reagan. Most people would concede that at least one person on the list did a good job as president, yet none appear to have had the top 1% IQ to get into a "top" school today.

Not that intelligence isn't important to success at work; for most jobs there is a threshold level of intelligence that is necessary to perform that job. Beyond that level, more intelligence is helpful but many other things come into play. If the student has the threshold IQ, then other types of abilities (e.g., interpersonal and intrapersonal) and hard work are much more important to ultimate success than stunning intellect.

Sociologist Steven Goldberg provides a good analogy: "In most occupations, academic ability plays the same role in determining success that weight plays in determining the success of offensive tackles in the National Football League. The heaviest tackle is not necessarily the best. In fact the correlation between weight and performance among offensive tackles is probably quite small. Factors other than weight are decisive. But to have even a chance of getting the job, you had better weigh at least 300 pounds."[41]

So from a college admissions standpoint, the task is to determine what level of IQ is necessary to be qualified intellectually for a career.[42] In very few if any jobs is a top 1 or 2% IQ that helpful; perhaps if one seeks a career as a quantum physicist or a Supreme Court justice. Hyperselectivity in admissions, if it is to exist at all, should be left to the graduate level. It has no place at the undergraduate level. The goal should be to maximize access to all who are qualified, not exclude as many of the qualified as possible.

## One Size Doesn't Fit All

Jobs vary in the mix of abilities necessary for success. The mix to be a good doctor is different from the mix to be a good lawyer is different from the mix to be a good first grade teacher is different from the mix to be a good mechanic, and so on and so forth.

Students also vary in their mix of abilities. For example, I have been around several individuals who have made a living as professsional musicians. However, I clearly do not have the musical aptitude to consider such a career. In fact, I got fired as a student by my sixth grade piano teacher. Luckily I am good with numbers and ideas; so I've been able to do okay in finance, law, and research.

But people do not just differ on abilities. It's also their interests. As Jim Collins[43] (and my parents) has advised, just because you seem genetically wired for a job and people will pay you a lot of money to do it doesn't mean you should do it.

Finally, and as the Puritan founders would argue most importantly, there is the call of God. "God doth call every man and woman ... to serve him in some particular employment in this world, both for their own and the common good...The Great Governor of the world hath appointed every man to his proper post and province."[44]

So given that people vary and job requirements vary, how does the existing higher education system work? Charles Murray answers by posing a hypothetical:

> Imagine that America had no system of postsecondary education and you were made a member of a task force assigned to create one from scratch. Ask yourself what you would think if one of your colleagues submitted this proposal:
>
> *First, we will set up a common goal for every young person that represents educational success. We will call it a BA. We will then make it difficult or impossible for most people to achieve this goal. For those who can, achieving the goal will take four years no matter what is being taught. We will attach an economic reward for reaching the goal that often has little to do with the content of what has been learned. We will lure large numbers of people, who do not possess adequate ability or motivation, to try to achieve the goal and then fail. We will then stigmatize everyone who fails to achieve it.*[45]
>
> What I have just described is the system we have in place. There must be a better way.

Murray is right, there is a better way. As Proverbs 6:22 admonishes: "Train up a child in the way he should go [and in keeping with his individual gift or bent], and when he is old he will not depart from it." Rather than trying to force every student into the same educational mold, higher education should be designed to maximize the individual student's God-given abilities and interests, or to move a few millennia away from Solomon into the 1970s—"Different Strokes for Different Folks."

We need a higher education industry that provides variety because needs differ. However from the standpoint of an individual college, you must guard against trying to serve everyone. It is impossible to do well. In fact, the needs of one segment may be in total conflict with the needs of another. Trying to be all things to all people is a recipe for failure. Define a target segment that is big enough to be economically viable, and then tailor your value proposition to that segment.

## Ignore the Prestige-Oriented Student (and Parents)

As long as the focus is on value (high quality at a reasonable price), there are numerous potential target markets for a Better/Cheaper College. However, there is one segment that must be avoided—the prestige-driven (exclusivity at a high price). In the eyes of many, higher education is a way to improve, protect, and visibly display one's status. In *Declining by Degrees*, Tom Wolfe wrote:

> Getting into Harvard! The pandemic known as college mania had just begun to show its true virulence that year (1988). Parents in large cities and many smaller ones had begun succumbing in droves to the mad compulsion to cover their families with glory by getting their children into the very best colleges as rated each fall by the *U.S. News & World Report*...parents caught up in the madness of it all were utterly consumed by a single passion: *getting in*...getting their children into a college whose name would go *bingo*! in every listener's head...preferably Harvard, or if not Harvard, Yale; or if not Yale, Princeton; or if not Harvard, Yale, or Princeton, then...
>
> On and on raged the fever. *Getting in!* Getting in become the be-all and the end-all. All else—education, character (a word that had become as anachronistic at colleges as cohabitation), conceptual thinking, work discipline, God, Freedom, and Immortality (Kant's trinity)—all else was a mopping up operation.[46]

Several colleges have been extremely successful financially by catering to these prestige-driven shoppers. They are able to charge far above market prices because of their exclusivity, a level of academic selectivity that is vastly above what is necessary from an educational perspective. These colleges limit their size, yet aggressively market to build demand to extremely high levels. While this leads to much higher sales expense per student (again, admissions is the education euphemism for sales), it is more than offset by higher revenue per student. On top of that, the prestige-driven segment of the market often equates price with quality (or maybe just likes to engage in conspicuous consumption).

The end result is that price is extremely high because that's what the market will bear. The students pay a very high price in return for hopefully a good education but more importantly status. Even if they realize the students can get the same quality education elsewhere at a significantly lower price, they still come to the elite college for access to the appropriate social/professional network and a high-profile credential that will guarantee success in life. In effect, the student and their parents are trying to buy their way to the head of the class of life.

The prestige strategy has proven a financial gold mine for many colleges. The college gets a great student to pay a lot for the right to associate with other great students. Since they are non-profits, they then spend all the difference between what they charge and what their services actually cost to produce. They then argue that this high spending is a sign that the quality of their education is superior to their lower priced competitors. On top of that, they aggressively raise money to build endowments so that their profligacy can be supported into perpetuity.

This strategy has worked well for several colleges, but the good news for society as a whole is that it doesn't work for the parent and their child. Benefits from exclusivity are rarely reaped by the prestige consumer because actual success in life goes as much to the academically well qualified as academically super. At the graduate school level, graduates reap benefits from high prestige when pursuing a career in academics. Outside academics, there are career benefits from going to a high-prestige professional school in some areas, like business and law, but not in others, like education and medicine.

However, looking at undergraduate education, studies have shown that the prestige of the institution has, at most, minimal impact on its graduates' economic future if you control for IQ and family socioeconomic status.[47] E.g., let's take a National Merit Scholar from an upper middle income family in Boston. His economic future post graduation will be no better as a result of going to Harvard than the University of Massachusetts. Some like literary critic, William Deresiewicz (former Yale English professor and holder of five degrees from Columbia) go further and argue that there are actually significant disadvantages to an elite college education beyond the high price tag.⁴⁸

Even though they can't really guarantee financial and social success to their students, many colleges have done extremely well selling to the prestige segment. There are enough students (or parents) in the prestige-driven segment of the market to allow several medallion brand colleges to do incredibly well financially. Even colleges that aren't that exclusive academically have successfully tapped into the prestige segment (you're selling to the Trophy Generation and their parents). Given the financial success of the many colleges in this segment, there is a real temptation to go after this prestige segment.

## Don't Do It

First, the prestige segment is already saturated. As evidenced by the overall market dominance of state research universities, most students are value driven. Further the size of the prestige segment may shrink significantly with the recent societal trend away from prestige to value shopping.⁴⁹ Second, what the prestige segment wants—intellectual and social status at high prices—is not what a Better/Cheaper College offers. Third, the values of the prestige segment are not consistent with those of the Better/Cheaper College and the liberal education it seeks to provide. Georgetown Professor Patrick Deneen elaborates.

> A liberal education—most often pursued in the context of a religiously-affiliated college or land-grant university—was originally an education in self-governance, moral restraint, and acknowledgment of the limits of human power and preparation for life in a family and a community.... liberal education did not so much "liberate" students from the limits of their backgrounds as it reinforced a basic teaching embedded deeply within their own cultural tradition, namely an education in limits. Often this conception of limits—conceived most often as based in morality or virtue—was drawn from the religious traditions of the particular institution. Most classical liberal arts institutions founded within a religious tradition required not only knowledge of the great texts of the tradition—including and especially the Bible— but corresponding behavior that constituted a kind of

"habituation" in the virtues learned in the classroom. Compulsory attendance at chapel or Mass, parietal rules, adult-supervised extracurricular activities, and required courses in moral philosophy (often taught by the president of the respective college) sought to integrate the humanistic and religious studies of the classroom with the daily lives of the students.

Such a form of "liberal education" would be objectionable across the board in today's society—by faculty, administrators, students and even parents. To the extent that it would neglect the education in success—the formation of a character that is capable of living anywhere and doing nearly anything demanded by the competitive global marketplace (even economically eviscerating the very sorts of communities from which a student originally came), it would fail to provide the sort of result that is demanded by the global society and by the consumers and providers within the elite institutions. A school that insisted that the mark of success would be achieved by students who returned to their home communities where they sought to contribute the benefits of their education, or who understood that a good life was constituted by the formation of sound families in settled communities, would certainly be regarded as some kind of fantastical and risible institution. Students at the schools where I have taught—Princeton and Georgetown—uniformly have absorbed the belief that a mark of failure would be to return to their home state or town upon graduation (unless that happened to be one of five or so large American or international cities). Almost certainly demand would decrease, jeopardizing a school's rankings and all the attendant benefits that come from such prestige.[50]

A Better/Cheaper College can be designed for many target markets, but it must avoid catering to the prestige shopper. Better/Cheaper's purpose is to provide a useful education for the benefit of both student and society. This isn't what the prestige shopper wants.

# 6

# Define a Value Proposition

After identifying a target market, the next step in designing a business model is to define a value proposition.[51] A college's value proposition is the set of benefits it offers students to satisfy their needs. In creating a value proposition, focus on the needs of your target market. The value proposition needs to match the needs of your students.

The value proposition for CELS (my hypothetical $7,376 Ivy) on p. 131 is an example of a value proposition aimed at a broad section of the traditional, residential undergraduate college student market. While an excellent value proposition, it is one of several viable value propositions for that target market. Because there are many market segments, there are many potential value propositions.

No matter what your target market, there are three points to keep in mind. One, you must be able to deliver the promised value. Two, don't include things in your value proposition that add benefits that your target market doesn't care about. Three, don't be easy.

## Must Haves for Any Value Proposition

***One you can deliver.*** Former Harvard President Derek Bok warns against "a tendency to accept goals without pausing to consider whether it is possible to achieve them within the time available in the curriculum."[52] Similarly, Thomas Sowell warns of education's tendency to focus "on the *desirability* of doing something to the complete exclusion of the question of our *capability* of doing it... No doubt it would be far more desirable to travel through the air like Superman, instead of inching along in a traffic jam. But that is no reason to leap off skyscrapers. Our education system is full of the results of leaping off skyscrapers."[53] A good value proposition does not go beyond the capabilities of student and college.

***Don't add benefits your students don't want.*** Providing benefits your students don't want increases your costs without improving benefits. For example, the value proposition for a residential college needs to provide a vibrant student life. This costs money. For CELS, the cost of providing student life is over $2,000 per student. While this is a vital part of the CELS value proposition that its target market wants, the commuter student market has no interest in student life. So if you are targeting the commuter student, don't spend money providing student life. You can then provide the commuter student market with a quality education for about $6,000, rather than $8,000.

***Don't be easy.*** Because students are the primary workers in the production of their education, it is vital to make them work. The amount of work that students put into college has declined dramatically. In 1961 the average full-time college student devoted 40 hours per week to academics. By 2004 it had dropped to 27 hours per week.[54] A little of this drop may be justifiable due to improved technology, e.g., it takes less time to "type" a term paper, but most of the reduced effort leads to a drop in learning. While being easy may make some students happy while in school, it fails to prepare them for life after school. The students don't learn what they should from their academics, and they also are taught self-destructive habits.

Today's American college students are more narcissistic than prior students. Their mean score on the Narcissistic Personality Index approaches that of celebrity movie stars, musicians, and reality show winners.[55] Often these students "have a sense of entitlement—often astonishing to others—which they consider as simply congruent with their special status."[56] Colleges should reduce these student's narcissism, not reinforce it.

A lack of standards also hurts good students. Good students want to be pushed to prepare for life. When the bar is set so low that slackers can slide over it, good students are not getting what they want—a good education. In addition, when bad students can graduate from a college, the value of a degree from that college declines. This hurts good students who hold the same degree. The value of their credential is less than it should be because bad students are allowed to graduate.

The nature and height of the academic bar should depend upon the student's ability and desired outcomes. It must be set high enough to insure that graduates can perform the jobs that they are being educated for. The college is certifying to society that this is the case. Colleges should take this responsibility very seriously. The bar must be at the right height, and students must go over the bar. Students should get passing grades only if they do the work and know the material.

## What Type of Education Do You Provide?

There are three basic types of education—vocational, general technical (e.g., critical thinking, teamwork, leadership, etc.) and liberal. (What accreditors refer to as general education is a combination of liberal and general technical education). The amount of each that you offer depends on your value proposition. Some programs are vocational—e.g., plumbers and urologists, but at the bachelor's level, programs should offer a mix of the three.

Let's take a look at what both students and employers want to see as learning outcomes from an undergraduate education. Employers want students with job relevant skills. In fact, only 15% recruit students with liberal arts degrees.[57] This emphasis on learning vocational skills is also held by prospective students. 91% want them. However, both prospective students and employers want students to develop more general technical skills.

Michigan State University's Annual Recruiting Trends Survey asks business and human resource people what they expect from a college graduate. Those surveyed said college graduates need more of the following.

- Flexibility and adaptability, as well as the ability to live with ambiguity and change
- Teamwork skills and group work activities, less territorial focus
- Independence and self-starter skills, as well as taking personal responsibility for getting the job done
- Organizational skills and time management abilities
- Higher level technical skills and experience to handle the wider range of skills required
- Communication skills, especially interpersonal abilities and sensitivity to customer relations
- Project management orientation and entrepreneurial orientation, as well as an ability to think outside the box
- Eagerness for lifelong learning and more interest in cross training.

In a George Dehne Associates[58] survey, college-bound students were asked what "skills" they expect to gain from their college experience. The list was varied and broad.

- Communication skills: including the ability to write and speak effectively and persuasively. 96%
- Professional skills: the traits, skills and talents needed in all professions. They range from time-management skills to how to manage yourself in a job interview. 94%
- Lifelong-learning skills: how to find information and how to research new areas of interest. 91%
- Social skills: the ability to communicate effectively and with poise in a variety of settings, develop positive relationships with others, and establish your own personal style. 92%
- Intellectual skills: problem solving, critical thinking, reasoning and analytical skills. 91%
- Leadership and management skills: the ability to lead, manage, motivate, and persuade people in an effective manner. 87%
- Personal management skills: being able to manage financial, social, physical and recreational life after college. 89%
- Multicultural skills: the ability to interact and appreciate diverse cultural and racial groups. 81%
- Values clarification: the identification and clarification of your own set of values and ethics. 81%
- Change skills: the flexibility needed for change and the ability to identify and create opportunities. 84%
- Citizenship skills: involvement and understanding of the democratic process, community service and the further development of a social consciousness. 75%

When you compare the two lists, the only real difference is that employers weren't interested in personal management skills, citizenship skills and values clarification. This isn't surprising since they relate primarily to the non-job aspects of life. However, overall the similarities are striking.

The fact that a college focuses on the acquisition of useful skills doesn't mean that students aren't learning foundational concepts. Often, it is impossible to acquire a skill without understanding foundational concepts. Without exposure to the major values and how they have played out in history, how can a student develop personal ethics? Without a sound knowledge of the Constitution, how can a student be a good citizen? Etc.

Many ITC members from the liberal arts strongly object to the vocational component of undergraduate education. However, most students want a vocational component. Employers are in agreement. Having a vocational component doesn't need to come at the expense of liberal education and general technical education. There is plenty of room for all three in a four-year undergraduate program.

For example, CELS has very robust liberal education and general technical education components. 56 credit hours are specifically devoted to liberal education and general technical education. This is a far greater emphasis on liberal education and general technical education than is seen today at most liberal arts colleges and still leaves 64 hours for vocational training. .

CELS value proposition is to provide students with a broad vocational education that includes 1) technical skills for entry-level jobs (or to start graduate school if necessary) in their chosen fields; 2) base knowledge to be general managers early in their careers; 3) an understanding of the institutional, intellectual, and social histories of their chosen vocations; as well as 4) its ethical and social responsibilities. This can be done within the remaining 64 hours. In fact, Engineering Science is the only vocational major that uses the full 64 hours. All the other majors take about 40 hours, leaving almost a full year of electives. For those wanting a humanities education, there is a 54 hour Letters & Civilization major, but that includes a 20 hour minor in one of the vocational fields.

## How Long to Graduate?

In designing a value proposition, you need to realize that tuition isn't the only cost to the student (or parent). Higher education also has a large opportunity cost. What could students do with their time if they were not in college? For a student who can make $40,000 a year upon graduation, the opportunity cost of spending one more year in college is $40,000.

Today it takes too long to get a college education. Several education experts have argued for two major reforms.[59] First, reduce the length of a bachelor's degree from four years to three. Second, make an Associate's degree, not a Bachelor's the requisite education for many careers. They argue this would dramatically decrease the cost of college without having any impact on quality. In most cases, I agree. I'll go one step further and argue that high school should be three years not four. Now these changes would be great for society and the student, but not for the industry. So I'm not holding my breath.

However, there are some things that colleges can do within the existing system. First, they can encourage academically qualified students to skip their last year of high school (graduate early or get a GED) and enroll. Second, they can structure their course offerings so that any interested student can take an accelerated schedule and earn an Associates in 15 months and a bachelors in 30. This is very easy to do with summer school and online classes.

While accelerated scheduling doesn't decrease tuition costs since student's still have to take the required 120 credit hours, it does substantially reduce opportunity costs. Rather than missing 4 years of pay, the student only misses three. At many colleges today it is possible to graduate in three years, but it is rarely encouraged. In fact, many colleges do not offer enough class sections of required courses to allow students to graduate in three years. Some even limit the availability of course offerings so much as to make some students stay five years in order to get a bachelors degree.

Some object that shortening time to degree would be harmful to students because it reduces "socialization" benefits to students. True, a major aspect of some value propositions is socialization. Socialization historically has been a major part of the residential undergraduate college value proposition. Students are to leave the safety of home and grow up into independent adults while in college. In their marketing campaigns, most private colleges today give lip service to this maturation element of the value proposition, but most do not deliver. In fact, undergraduate colleges are often criticized for encouraging dependency rather than independency.[60]

Given the ability to create a separate mini-society, residential colleges can include maturation as a major part of their value proposition. However, this doesn't mean you need to take four years in college. Much of maturation is informal. The formal aspects don't take that much time to deliver. For example, Army ROTC provides vastly more formal leadership training in one month than most colleges do over four years.[61]

## Liberal Education in the 21st Century

Liberal education should be major part of any bachelor's degree. There are a lot of ways to approach teaching the "know right" part of a liberal education. One doesn't need to go back to the Harvard curriculum of 1825, or its more recent variation, The Great Books. A liberal education is not synonymous with a particular curriculum and certainly does not require four years. The goal of liberal education isn't for students to have a deep understanding of the "great minds" of civilization as seen in all the original texts. It is okay to use Cliff Notes for Plato. The purpose is to enable graduates "to perform justly, skillfully, and magnanimously, all the offices, both private and public."

The fundamental question in providing liberal education is what religious framework, virtues, or shared values to use as the underlying foundation. The whole idea of morality, particularly one that is metaphysically derived, poses a real problem for most secular colleges. Yet how can they provide a liberal education without any moral beliefs? Derek Bok suggests building moral education for undergraduates upon commonly shared values or what is sometimes referred to as Natural Law.

> Since ethical issues ultimately rest on values rather than provable facts, not all moral questions have definite answers. Still, all societies and major religions share certain basic moral beliefs, such as a general disapproval of lying, cheating, breaking promises, and using violence against others. With the help of these common values, careful analysis can often lead to reasonably clear conclusions. Even when moral disagreements seem insoluble, further thought can sometimes produce an imaginative course of action that will avoid the ethical difficulties while still achieving the ends of everyone involved.
>
> Moral disagreements do occur in which all attempts at reason fail to yield an acceptable result.... Even when truly intractable issues arise, close analysis can at least dispose of much shoddy thinking and thereby clarify the nature of the underlying dispute. Students can gradually overcome the easy relativism that often characterizes undergraduate discussions of ethical questions as they come to observe that

some arguments are more firmly grounded in fact and reason than others. In this way, they may gain in understanding even when they cannot ultimately agree on the solution.

The Natural Law approach focuses on ethics and downplays metaphysics. The benefit of the Natural Law approach is that it provides a good basis for defining how people of differing views can live together. However, this strength is also its weakness. It focuses on universality and ignores plurality. Moreover, a liberal education that stops at the level of Natural Law is one that many students will find intellectually and spiritually superficial and sterile—a flimsy foundation for life.

A very different approach from the Natural Law College is the Church College. Several Christian colleges have been successful in making liberal education a vital part of their value proposition.[62] To a great extent they could be viewed as colleges that are also churches. They hold to specific religious views, include them in their curriculum, and enforce clear codes of behavior. They stress both corporate worship and individual spiritual development as parts of their value proposition.

These Church Colleges appeal to specific target markets. In fact the liberal education portion of their value proposition is so strong that they can attract students even though their tuition is much higher than public colleges and often the vocational education they provide is seen as inferior to public flagships. The Church College obviously doesn't appeal to all students. That's okay. They don't have to attend.

There is a middle ground between the Church College and the Natural Law College. A liberal education could be grounded in a variety of variations of what could be referred to American Natural Law ("We hold these truths to be self-evident, that all men are created equal, that they are endowed by their Creator with certain unalienable Rights, that among these are Life, Liberty and the pursuit of Happiness"), or the American Tradition (representing a "national consensus of shared values that are essentially secular, but … in harmony with the common theistic and moral teachings of Protestants, Catholics, and Jews."[63] or the "American Order."[64]

The American Order is largely a product of the combination of Christianity (particularly the Reformation) and the Enlightenment (particularly the Anglo-Scottish). As a result, there are numerous more particular views that are consistent with American Order, but are often in conflict with each other. To force a person to follow one of these more particular views is actually inconsistent with the American Order's emphasis on individual religious freedom. So an American Order college would provide theistic and moral teaching at a broad level (e.g., the Apostles Creed), require basic moral behavior, and encourage spiritual development. However sectarian religious training and practice would be provided by church and para-church organizations, with participation at the individual student's discretion. CELS takes this approach.

Whatever your approach to teaching "know right" to students, it is pointless if they ultimately do not "do right." If they desire, colleges can do an excellent job of teaching any student to "know right." It is another matter to educate so that students "do right." Colleges can encourage and inspire students to "do right" through a variety of means: inspirational/religious programming, positive peer pressure, proscribed and prescribed rules of conduct, and role models. The opportunities for helping students "do right" are limited in an online setting. But at a minimum, any college can model "do right" in its corporate actions and the individual actions of its faculty and staff.

Undergraduate residential education is where there is the most room for education to "do right." Here you can literally have habituation in values. You don't have to be Bob Jones University (no contemporary Christian music, chaperone required for dates, etc.). But, you don't want to be DuPont University (Tom Wolfe's fictional amalgam of today's elite colleges where the pursuit of material goods, physical pleasure, and social standing are the driving forces of student life and the university is indifferent and enabling). There are a lot of viable options in between.

When you combine the multiple approaches to educating in "know right" with the numerous options to educate in "do right," there are many viable value propositions. The key is to deliver a value proposition that is appealing to your target market. This value proposition should be in keeping with the values of the college, but it also has economic ramifications. Too focused and the market is limited; too broad, and you lose students because you are not sufficiently differentiated from your competitors.

# Part III: Designing a Better/Cheaper College

# 7

# Pick the Right Activities to Perform

A college has to perform a variety of activities to deliver on its value proposition. If you fail, then you cannot provide the desired benefits to your students. If you do too many activities (or even too much of a good activity), costs will increase without an offsetting increase in benefits. Proper selection of activities to perform is vital in designing a Better/Cheaper College.

## You Need a Good Set of Plans to Build a Good Product

A well-designed curriculum is foundational to both improving student learning and lowering costs. To design a curriculum, you need to decide what it is your students need to be able to do, then decide what combination of content knowledge, skills, and experience is necessary for students to achieve these abilities.[65] The ultimate goal is for the student to acquire abilities useful in life after college. If acquiring an ability requires prolonged experience, then you are seriously constrained in developing that ability in a formal educational setting. However, some abilities can be significantly developed in a formal educational setting. For other abilities, formal education can provide the knowledge and skills that are necessary for the ability, with the realization that the ability itself can only be developed through real life experience.

Once you have decided the knowledge/skills/abilities that students are to have at graduation, then you design courses (and sometimes extracurricular experiences) to teach them. The curriculum represents the combination of courses that insures that the student will graduate with the desired knowledge/skills/abilities.

Unfortunately, most college curriculums today have massive gaps. As the earlier discussion of the problems with general education curriculum demonstrates, this really isn't seen as a major problem by many within higher education. If the purpose of college is learning for learning's sake, it doesn't matter much what you learn. An extreme example is the undergraduate curriculum that was in place at Brown University from 1969 to 2009. It required that students take 30 courses over 4 years in absolutely anything.

In addition to requiring the right courses, the curriculum should not require students to take courses that are not relevant to their future life. (Thirty years after the fact, I still don't get why all business majors need to take calculus.) Students should not be required to waste their time and money taking irrelevant courses. Even worse is the stultifying effect these courses often have on students. They come to college excited about college as a foundation to their future and are immediately faced by an indecipherable mess of often pointless required classes. Courses should not be required unless they are relevant to one's life or career. You shouldn't make students take classes they're not interested in unless they really do need them. In addition, a college should strive to make the required courses as interesting as possible. It's in these classes that students intrinsic motivation is usually the lowest.

Good curriculum design requires that the right courses are required, that the wrong courses aren't required, and that interdependencies between courses be properly managed. For example, a student needs to take a foundational course before a more advanced course. What a student learned in the foundational course should influence what is taught in the advanced course and how it is taught. Foundational courses provide initial exposure to content knowledge and skills (and in some cases may give students basic abilities). Advanced courses then sustain and reinforce the knowledge and skills learned in the foundational course as they also expand and extend knowledge and skills and give students more advanced abilities.

These interdependencies are a major issue in designing a college curriculum. The interdependency problem in curriculum design is also found in any type of complex product design (cars, computers, buildings, etc.) where the product is made up of multiple component parts. In his recent book *Disrupting Class: How Disruptive Innovation Will Change the Way the World Learns*,[*] Clayton Christenson draws on principles of product design to illustrate the problem caused by interdependencies in education.

> When someone changes one piece in a product that has an interdependent architecture, necessity requires comple-

---

[*] Copyright 2008 Reproduced with the permission of the McGraw-Hill Companies.

mentary changes in other pieces. Customizing a product or service, as a result, becomes complicated and expensive. Many of these interdependencies are not predictable so all pieces must be designed interactively. Customizing a product whose architecture is interdependent requires a complete redesign of the entire product or service.[66]

Not only are customized products extremely expensive to build, but the end product often is of inferior quality to a standardized product. So full customization is rarely an appropriate approach to designing a complex product. Ph.D. programs are the only places you need a high level of customization in higher education.

The opposite approach of customization is standardization. Standardization can solve the interdependency problem but treats each student the same. For colleges that only offer highly specialized degrees, standardization may be the answer.

However, it doesn't work well in the typical undergraduate setting. Most colleges are trying to provide an education to students with a variety of career and personal interests. The solution is mass customization. Done right, mass customization combines the cost and quality advantages of standardization with a product meeting the more personal needs of each student.

On the surface, a majority of colleges appear to use mass customization. They may have some required general education courses (Composition or American History) and numerous different majors. Often one course is listed as a prerequisite to another; some are taken freshman year, others are only for seniors, etc. Unfortunately mass customization hasn't really worked in practice because colleges do not seriously spend time identifying the interdependencies in the curriculum, much less designing a curriculum that addresses them. At most colleges, mass customization is a façade.

For mass customization you must have modular architecture. The components (courses) must fit and work together in well-defined ways. This can happen only if the interface between components (courses) is predictable. Designing with modular architecture takes much more time, money, and discipline than the higgledy-piggledy approach most colleges use. But over time, it pays off in massive improvements in both quality and cost.

## Undergraduate Curriculum

The undergraduate curriculum has three basic parts. First is a general educational core that teaches general knowledge/skills/abilities (e.g., defining the Bill of Rights/performing basic statistical analysis/problem solving). Then there is a major for learning more specific knowledge/skills/abilities, and further developing general knowledge/skills/abilities by applying them in specific career situations. Finally there are a few electives that students can take to either learn technical knowledge and skills outside of their majors or for personal enjoyment.

A major should teach a set of technical knowledge/skills/abilities that matches up with career opportunities. Kent Brockman, television news man in the *Simpsons*, once defined hard economic times when he reported, "things aren't as happy as they used to be down here in the unemployment office. Joblessness is no longer just for philosophy majors—useful people are starting to feel the pinch." Perhaps Kent is a little harsh on people with philosophy degrees, but the concept of an undergraduate philosophy major doesn't make practical sense. Majors should be designed to help people be useful.

Students must at a minimum achieve the level of technical abilities necessary to perform tasks expected of an entry-level employee. The technical knowledge/skills/abilities set should be reasonably broad so as to allow multiple initial job options and make it easier to switch jobs as a career progresses. In addition to learning career-specific technical skills, students need be familiar with current trends as well as the institutional, social, and intellectual history of their careers. They need to be particularly aware of the ethical and social responsibilities of their work. And as Michael Clifford suggests, "How about helping them develop passion for their work?"[67]

Having career-focused majors doesn't mean that students aren't learning basic concepts from the arts and sciences. Rather, it means no traditional arts and sciences disciplinary majors. These majors just don't fit with the "education for a better life" philosophy because they take an Ivory Tower approach by focusing on in-depth learning of one academic discipline.

Let's take two of the most popular arts and sciences majors—psychology and biology. Some things a student learns as a psychology major are foundational to useful abilities, but the major avoids teaching these abilities. Many psychology students are interested in working as some type of counselor, yet most psychology departments do not offer a single counseling course. Other students are interested in jobs requiring some psychology-based abilities (e.g., communications, public affairs, and management) but have no need for courses like Abnormal Psychology or Physiological Psychology.

Most students majoring in biology are not interested in the discipline in itself. Rather, they want to learn foundational technical knowledge that can be applied someday in a specific profession, such as being a medical doctor. In an article in *The New England Journal of Medicine*, Jules Dienstig, dean for medical education at Harvard Medical School, discussed the current state of undergraduate pre-med education.

> Unfortunately, current college courses that fulfill admissions requirements are not adequately focused on human biology; the topics covered in many courses in chemistry, physics, mathematics, and even biology are so removed from human biologic principles that they offer little value to the pre-medical—or advanced human biology—student and steal time and attention from more relevant science preparation... A reasonable prescription for efficiency and economy would involve refocusing, increasing relevance, setting a higher standard, and encouraging the design of more interdisciplinary premedical science courses... A sick patient does not represent a biochemistry problem, an anatomy problem, a genetics problem, or an immunology problem.

Academic disciplines can provide very useful knowledge and skills, but they are a bad organizing framework for a college major. Majors need to provide students what they need for their futures. For example, in CELS there isn't a Political Science or Economics major, rather a Public Affairs major; and the Science and Technology major is designed to provide the prerequisites for medical school or the breadth to teach in high school or work in a technology-based business.

## Make it Personal

While the delivery of courses is generally best done through large classes or via technology, it is vital that education be made personal to the student. Making it personal gives students the best education possible through tailoring the college's curriculum and extracurriculum to the needs of the individual student. Making it personal also gets the students more engaged with college. Engaged students work harder and are more likely to persist in the face of challenges. There are three strategies to making it personal: quality personal interactions between student and the college's faculty and employees, strong connections among students, and high quality advising.

***Personal interactions with students.*** Quality interaction between the student and the college is the responsibility of all employees. An obvious focal point is the interaction between instructor and student in a course. An instructor's attitude as to the importance of students as people comes across in what the instructor says and does with the whole class. In addition, while one-to-one interactions between instructor and student are a small part of the interaction in most courses, when they do occur they should be done well. Further, in the residential college setting, it is important that faculty are regularly involved in the life of the college (e.g., attend concerts, sporting events, student organizations, etc.) and interact informally with students. This doesn't take much effort on the faculty's part (someone who really wants to be on the faculty of a residential undergraduate college should find this pleasure, not work) and really makes the students see the college as people rather than an uncaring machine.

It's not just the faculty who are responsible for making it personal. Many administrative and staff jobs include a lot of interpersonal interaction with students. Not doing them well alienates students and is inexcusable.

Michael Clifford gives some examples of this from Grand Canyon University.

> On the online side of things, we offer complete support to the students. We have a large call center that offers 24/7 support. Students can talk to an enrollment, academic, or financial adviser any time day or night. If they need technical help, it's available, even if the issue is related to Microsoft Outlook or any application they need to use for their course work.
>
> We do their entire financial planning, loan documents, payment plans, structuring their whole financial package. We will take care of getting their transcripts. The academic

advisor puts together the whole degree program for each student, explaining every detail.

This high level of customer service extends to our land-based campus as well. When we first took ownership of the school, we were inundated with students coming in with complaints. They'd say things like, "I've been to the business office five times in two weeks and they still don't know when I'm going to get my meal card working." It was a mess.

One evening we had a female student who had locked herself out of her campus apartment on a rainy night. She ran across campus in the rain to get to the business office before it closed at 5:00 PM. When she got there, it was exactly 5:00 PM, but the doors were already locked. She could see two people still in the office and knocked on the door to get their attention. She begged them to help her and they ignored her. This girl who was paying thousands of dollars a year for her education, plus thousands more for her housing, couldn't get the customer service she deserved. We ended up firing the two people who ignored her needs.

Customer service at Grand Canyon means responding quickly, no matter what time it is, and then putting processes in place to ensure the same problem never arises again.

**Other students.** Making it personal also involves creating an environment where students form strong relationships with their peers. The longer the program and the more residential its nature, the more important these relationships are. Students taking one online course don't need to bond, while students in a four-year degree program at a residential college benefit from developing relationships with other students.

Creating these relationships is important, but low cost to the college because the students are doing almost all the "work"; it's students taking time with other students. The college's role is primarily designing a system where student-to-student relationships flourish. This does not require small classes and lots of student development professionals. Having lots of small classes is a very expensive, and often ineffective, way to build community. Instead, big classes with small cohorts build community better than small classes with large cohorts, and at a significantly lower cost. This is the approach long taken by major law schools who divide incoming first year students into sections of about 100. Students then take all their first year courses only with students in their section. While class size is relatively large, community is created because it is the same 100 people in each class.

When small cohorts are combined with teaching techniques like Team Based Learning,[68] community among students is naturally formed. While some student development professionals are necessary in a residential college setting, most colleges have too many. This drives up cost without adding any benefit.

*Advising.* One area that most colleges need to spend more money on is advising. For minimal additional cost, colleges can provide excellent career, academic, and personal advising. Top notch advising significantly increases the ability to customize education to the student, and increases student satisfaction and commitment.[69] But as former Harvard College Dean Harry Lewis points out, "The inadequacy of the advising system is one of the few matters on which deans, professors, and students agree."[70]

The advising problem is most complex for traditional-age undergraduates. Here students start with minimal-to-no knowledge of potential careers; limited knowledge of their own abilities, interests, and rewards they value; and a large number of options to choose from. On top of that, they are making a huge life stage transition from adolescent to adult. So there is need for a lot of advising on all three fronts—career, academic, and personal. Ironically, while just about everybody is unhappy with current undergraduate advising systems, the solution is straightforward and relatively inexpensive.

The key is to create a structured, integrated, general advising process that takes students from matriculation to post-graduation employment. If the process is designed well, delivery is relatively simple. On the personal side, most issues are life-stage transition related and are fairly common to most students. Some students may have personal problems that don't fit well into a general advising process. It is best to approach these problems individually as they occur rather than try to fit them into the general advising process required for every student.

Initially, the focus of general advising is helping students get to know themselves. There are already several proven personal assessments that are available off-the-shelf and in online format. With good self-knowledge, students better develop their general skills for life and career. Self-knowledge is also vital to making good career decisions. After gaining self-knowledge, the advising focus shifts to making a broad career decision. Once again, proven off-the-shelf products are available for this purpose. This personal discovery and broad career counseling portion of general advising happens primarily in the first two years of college. If the college has a coherent curriculum, academic advising is simple the first two years since the number of options is limited.

Once a broad career decision has been made, career focused advising helps students look more in-depth at specific careers. Academic advising helps students pick courses and other experiences in pursuit of the student's career objectives. Academic advising becomes more difficult to provide for three reasons. First, the number of course options increases. Second, some of the courses may be customized so the student needs more guidance in which to take. Third, many activities like internships fall outside the control of the college and so cannot be standardized.

The final stage of the general advising process is career placement. Here the student needs help identifying and evaluating possible employers (or graduate schools). Often the college can also help in initiating the dialogue between student and their ultimate employer through career fairs and on-campus recruiting.

## Don't Spend Money on Activities That Don't Add Value

**Research.** Many universities spend a lot of money on research. Some may be funded by outside parties, but much is funded internally by the university. In fact, almost all research in the humanities, social sciences, and business is funded directly by the university. Producing research is a costly undertaking. Richard Vedder, founder of the Center for College Accountability and Productivity and distinguished professor of economics at Ohio University gives an example.

> Let us look at the senior faculty at a major flagship university, say the University of Michigan. Take a senior full professor of, say, political science or history. He or she probably makes a low six-digit salary which, with fringe benefits, may total $150,000 a year. Suppose this person teaches three classes over the course of an entire academic year.

Let us say the professor is writing a book that will take five years to complete (implying six or seven books over his/her career, a rather sizable output), and writes one fairly significant journal article each year as well. He/she also does some thesis supervision, advises a few students, and is on a couple of committees. This would be the typical life of a successful and relatively productive professor at a typical major university.

Now, let us cost it out. Starting with the professor's salary and benefits, let us allocate 40% for class instruction, 40% for research, and 20% for other—"service" and other quasi-instructional duties. In other words, the core instructional and research duties each cost $60,000 a year. If we assume the professor devotes his/her time equally to writing the journal article and the book, the journal article costs $20,000. Suppose, very optimistically, 500 people read it—that is $40 per person—not for a book, but for what is perhaps a 20-30 page paper. If, more realistically, 200 persons read it, the cost per reader is $100. The book will cost $100,000 ($20,000 × 5) in professorial time to prepare. Suppose 1,500 read it (a pretty good readership for an academic book). The cost per reader is $667.

And this does not consider all the overhead costs, academic support, etc. If we assume, as do federal granting agencies, that these costs are at least 50% of the direct salary costs, all the numbers above should be multiplied by at least 1.5. Thus the book will cost about $1,000 per reader. Moreover, suppose the professor is a historian writing the 20th account about some aspect of Andrew Jackson's life. Is it really worth it to society to spend $150,000 (plus book publication costs) to offer that 20th perspective?

[Moving significantly down the research pecking order, colleges still spend on research.] Research efforts are less in quantity and typically quality, and also far less in readership. Suppose an associate professor at Slippery Rock costs, with fringes, $100,000 a year, and she devotes 30% of her time to research, and writes one paper a year for an obscure academic journal and gives one paper at an equally obscure academic gathering—a rather typical occurrence. The journal article still costs at least $15,000, maybe $22,500 after indirect costs. Suppose, more realistically, that 50 people read the article in the Journal of Last Resort or its equivalent. The cost per reader is $450 for a paper that does not move the academic world, much less western civilization, one bit. If 25 people attend the session at the academic meeting that the paper is presented, that would be considered pretty good. If the paper costs $15,000 in salary and $22,500 in total to produce, the cost per listener at the meeting is $900. Outrageous! Yet no one does anything about it.[71]

From society's viewpoint, some research is beneficial and is worth more than it costs, some is beneficial but costs more than it is worth, and some just costs. From society's standpoint the first category should be funded and the later two not. Now in practice, distinguishing between the first and second category at times is difficult. Distinguishing between the first category and last category is easy, yet schools continue to fund research when its only potential outcome is total obscurity, even in the academic world.

Vedder's cost/benefit analysis looks at benefits from a societal standpoint. If you focus instead on costs and benefits to an individual college student, then spending money on research becomes much more questionable. Academic research may provide some benefits to society as a whole, but it provides little if any direct benefits to students, particularly undergraduates. Academic research is a public good.

Assume a researcher at University X makes a ground-breaking discovery in basic science that ultimately leads to a cure for cancer. University X students who have cancer benefit greatly from the research done at University X, but so do students with cancer at University Y or Z. In fact, so does somebody with cancer who dropped out of high school. The point isn't that research is a waste of money, it just that it doesn't confer any special benefits to students at the college where the discovery is made. I'm an alum of the college where the parking meter was invented (Oklahoma State), yet that has never gotten me out of a parking ticket!

While not adding benefits to students, research often actually reduces benefits. As about anybody who's been an undergraduate at a research university will testify, many faculty view undergraduate teaching as a distraction from their main research mission; this reflects in the quality of their teaching. So what should you do with an activity that costs a lot of money but detracts from value? How about eliminate it? At most colleges, faculty research activity should range from nonexistent to modest. Basically, it should be a job perk for interested and research qualified faculty, not an activity that's a significant part of the college's mission.

At universities that do have research as a significant part of their mission, care must be taken to insure that it is does not reduce the quality of undergraduate education and that it is not financially subsidized by money allocated for undergraduate education. (Using undergraduate funds to pay much of the cost of research is the common practice today. This isn't apparent to the public because universities have adopted an internal accounting convention that treats most university funded research costs as a cost of instruction).

I obtained my undergraduate degree from Oklahoma State and have spent all of my academic career as a professor there. We have been given a research mission by the State of Oklahoma. In fact, our school seal is a triangle with a glowing lamp in the middle. The lamp represents knowledge and the three sides are labeled Instruction, Research, and Extension. So we've definitely been tasked with a research mission. In addition, we also have a major public service mission (Extension).

As the name implies, public service like research is a public good. But unlike research, public service can often be provided at minimal additional cost to the college. (You're running the music series for students, why not sell tickets to the community? You have faculty with expertise who like to help in the community, so why not let them?) Public service also can help your image in the community and overall marketing. However, if not monitored regularly, the extra costs of this incidental public service can mount up.

Some universities go well beyond incidental public service. Any land grant university like Oklahoma State has a large-scale public service mission. Major state universities that are not land grant institutions generally also have a public service mission, but on a much lower scale. Some of the major private research universities have some public service mission. At other private colleges, there is a public service mission in the form of service to a religious denomination or a local community (i.e., there's an art museum or a music series). Historically, the conflicts between instruction and public service have been much less severe than the research/instruction conflict. However, some colleges that have taken on major public service activities like supporting a religious movement or a museum have found them a huge resource drain. Universities need to make sure that the cost of the public service mission is not paid for out of tuition or other revenues meant for instruction.

**Undersubscribed courses.** Another way to seriously reduce costs without impacting quality is to reduce the number of undersubscribed courses that are taught. An undersubscribed course is one where actual enrollment is below maximum enrollment, with maximum enrollment being the most students you can have in the course and still deliver it effectively. Maximum capacity depends on the nature of the course and teaching techniques.

In a place-based course, often class sections run well below maximum capacity. Because students need to be physically present at a set time, you can have student scheduling conflicts that necessitate offering multiple sections of the same course. Or sometimes a large enough classroom isn't available. Also at small colleges, you simply don't have enough students to reach capacity except in required general education classes. So to some extent, undersubscribed course are an unavoidable cost in place-based education.

However, the severity of the undersubscribed course problem is much greater than it needs to be. Many college administrators are very sloppy schedulers. This is partially caused by a lack of management skill, but due more to the Ivory Tower culture that doesn't value efficient use of money and time.

A great deal of the severely undersubscribed course problem comes from offering too many majors. You have classes that few students want because they are necessary in order to offer a major that few students want. Significant cost savings can be realized by eliminating or consolidating low enrollment majors.[72] On top of that, highly specialized, professional majors are generally inappropriate for undergraduates. Intellectually fragmented liberal arts majors are never appropriate at the undergraduate level. They do not prepare students for a career, and their intellectual narrowness is the antithesis of general education.

# 8

# Perform Activities the Right Way

Once you've decided which activities to perform, the next step in creating a business model is to determine the best way to perform these activities. While sometimes there is a cost/quality trade-off, most of the time the best way to perform an activity yields both high quality and low cost.

In this chapter we will look at some of the major activities a college performs, and the resources it needs in order to perform them. First, we'll look at instruction; second, the role of online delivery; third the proper utilization of physical assets; and finally the proper utilization of financial resources.

## Instructional Methods

Expensive instruction isn't the same as good instruction.[73] This is a myth the industry has aggressively promoted, but it simply isn't true. Instructional cost/quality win/win can be consistently achieved through the use of appropriate teaching techniques and technologies.

How a class is taught by faculty has a big impact on what is learned by students in that class. Unfortunately many classes are poorly taught. In his introduction to *Creating Significant Learning Experiences*, leading college instructional consultant L. Dee Fink comments on the general state of undergraduate teaching:

> Sitting in many courses gives one the feeling that teachers are doing an information dump. They have collected and organized all the information and ideas they have on a given topic and are dumping their knowledge onto (and they hope into) the heads of their listeners. When these courses are over, one has the scary feeling that the students are also about to engage in some information dumping of their own...Studies have been done where someone goes into college classrooms and measures what teachers actually do.

The number of times that a teacher even asks a question in a one-hour class period is remarkably low. In-depth, sustained discussions where students respond to other students as well as to the teacher are extremely rare.[74]

While most courses today may simply be content dumps, many are not. There are several different proven, teaching techniques available today. The "best" way to teach is contextual, based on the nature of subject matter, student and desired course outcomes. Since this isn't a book about how to be a teacher, I won't go into a detailed discussion of teaching techniques but will make three points that are important to the Better/Cheaper College.

First, active learning is better than passive learning. Passive learning is the receiving of information and ideas. It is what happens when one reads a text, listens to a lecture, or reads something on the internet. If learning doesn't go beyond passive learning, then the best the student is able to do is regurgitate the information back. They have not really learned anything.

Now passive learning is vital, but it is very limited learning. Active learning takes the information and ideas the student has passively received, and has the student engage with them. One way is through reflection. This is how students learn in lecture format classes. They take the material they are given, think about how it fits with other information, think about how it would work in practice, etc. A really good lecture gets students to do this. But more often than not, the student is left to reflect on his own.

In addition to reflection, the other major forms of active learning are experiences and observation. With experiences the student actually does what you want him/her to learn. Doing is particularly important in the acquisition of job focused skills. You don't want students to just be able to recite the steps of how to do it, you want them to able to do it. Generally the best way to learn how to do something is to be introduced to the idea, and then learn it by trying to apply the idea to realistic situations. This is why the case method used for decades by business schools is so effective for learning.

Second, appropriate use of technology makes a big difference. As will be discussed shortly, online education is having a huge impact today on the higher education industry. But technology can also have a major positive impact on traditional place-based education. Technology is particularly helpful for course management and for the "content dump" (e.g. video lectures) and "drill & kill" (e.g. programmed learning) components of instruction.

An example of the use of technology in ground based education is the two hour linear algebra class at Virginia Tech University.[75] This course is taken each year by 2,000 first-year students majoring in engineering, physical science, and mathematics. It had historically been taught in sessions of 40 students with twice weekly lectures and homework assignments. In 1999, this course was changed to an online delivery model with on-demand tutoring assistance. These materials can be studied at home or at an on-campus lab that is open 24/7 with faculty and peer tutors on-site. The results have been impressive. By 2001, the total cost per student had fallen from $91 to $21, and the pass rate grew from 80.5% to 87.25%. (For those wondering what happened to the $70 per student in savings, see the chapter on ITC profits).

Technology can also be used to let students have relatively complex, virtual experiences. For example, *The Business Strategy Game*, an online simulation, has been a mainstay in strategic management classes for over a decade. In it, student teams spend about thirty hours over the semester managing a "company" in head-to-head competition against companies run by other class members. Companies compete in a global market arena, selling branded and private-label athletic footwear in four geographic regions—Europe-Africa, North America, Asia-Pacific, and Latin America. Over 35,000 students a year now take part in this one simulation.[76]

Third, small classes are not inherently better than large classes. Colleges constantly talk about a low student/faculty ratio as if it is the hallmark of quality instruction. Since faculty costs per student credit hour is the biggest cost driver, having two or three times as many faculty as you need has a huge cost impact; all these additional faculty better add a lot to student learning.

Unfortunately, they don't. You get low student-faculty ratios two ways. One, faculty don't teach many classes a year. This is common in research-oriented schools. Say, rather than teaching four three-hour courses a semester (a common full teaching load for a non-researcher), faculty only teach two courses a semester and devote their remaining time to research. As a result, the research school needs two professors to do the instructional work of one professor.

Having the extra professor doubles the cost per student but does not have any impact on the quality of instruction.

The other way student faculty ratios are lowered is to have small classes. Colleges love to talk about the number of classes they offer with under twenty enrolled (this is a measure of quality used by the *U.S. News* rankings).[77] However, in most cases, small classes are no better than large classes from a learning standpoint. Ivy League schools run jumbo lecture classes a lot. Many are quite popular. The key is how well the course is designed and delivered, not how big the class is. Even the ritziest of the small liberal arts schools like Williams and Amherst regularly offer classes with over 40 enrolled. This is because from a pedagogical standpoint, you can do the same thing in a class of 140 students as a class of 30 students. The only difference is it will require marginally more[78] faculty time for course administration and grading, but this is irrelevant from a student learning standpoint.

The only time you need a small class is if the student's work product is highly customized, e.g. a field project or a senior paper. Given the amount of standard concepts to be mastered, there isn't room for many classes requiring custom work. In fact, as we discussed earlier, too much customization actually lowers quality.

The goal of most college courses, both undergraduate and in professional schools, is the learning of an established body of knowledge and skills. Custom seminars where students write and critique research papers are not a good way to do this. Rather high participation/application teaching techniques where multiple students examine and solve the same problem are vastly more effective for learning both basic content and higher level application skills. The classic example is the case method, long a staple in law schools and graduate business schools. More recently, Team Based Learning[79] has been used in a variety of disciplines, particularly medicine and business.

Team Based Learning is a variation of traditional case teaching in which small group discussion and all-class discussion are blended in a single class period. By working in five to seven person teams, students are forced to be actively involved in learning both content and application. A Team Based Learning class of 100 generates heavy student in-class involvement from all 100 students. A traditional class of 19 generates heavy student in-class involvement from relatively few, or even none. Yet the faculty cost per student of the small class is five times greater.

## Online Courses

Online education is already having a major impact on access. It has been used extensively by many universities over the last decade. From a technological and pedagogical perspective, it is a proven delivery mechanism.[80] The use of online has exploded in recent years, especially through the for-profit higher education industry. In 1986, around 2% of students were enrolled in for-profit higher education. Yet, by 2010 that figure had climbed considerably to nearly 2 million students; accounting for nearly 10% of all students enrolled in postsecondary education.[81]

In a recent survey of college administrators, the majority currently view online as educationally equivalent to face-to-face.[82] As with place-based education, the quality of online courses varies radically, as does their level of difficulty, depending on instructor and institution. Pedagogically, online is generally seen as a viable, although second best delivery mechanism, in courses designed to have a large amount of professor-to-student or student-to-student interaction. Online courses are equivalent to place-based delivery (some argue better) in courses built along the more common lecture/limited Q&A/individual paper/test format. Online is often viewed as better for courses stressing the learning and application of algorithms[83] A weakness of online is limited informal learning (e.g. learning from out-of-class conversations with classmates). In addition, online requires a more motivated and disciplined student. As a result, *online may not work well with immature students—e.g., the typical college freshman.*

Online delivery can greatly increase access. It removes geographic and time limits to access. Online delivery makes learning available when and where it is convenient for the student, not when and where it is convenient for the instructor or institution. Anyone with a connection to the Internet, anywhere, at any time can have access to a quality education.

Online also increases access by lowering the cost of going to college for many students. Even if tuition remains the same, total costs of going to school can go down significantly for many students.

No longer does the student need to leave their paid-for home and rent a dorm room. No longer do you have to forego working a well-paying paid job in order to go to get an advanced degree.

Online also makes it possible for schools to charge lower tuition because it costs the college less to provide instruction via online. While the costs of IT infrastructure can be high, they are usually substantially cheaper than the costs of a ground campus. Online can also offer substantial savings in faculty labor cost because it usually is more efficient in terms of faculty labor hours per student credit hours. After a course is designed, the online instructor's work is limited to grading, providing feedback, and answering questions. The amount of work involved is primarily a function of the number of students enrolled. In contrast, in a place-based class the amount of faculty effort involved is largely fixed, varying little with enrollment.

In terms of faculty time, it probably costs about two times more faculty hours per student FTE to teach a class of 20 on campus as opposed to online. Most online courses cap section size at 30. So when enrollment goes above 30, you have to add another section. From a cost standpoint, this means doubling your faculty costs. So the cost advantage of online begins to disappear. When enrollments are running over 90, place-based delivery may actually be cheaper than online.[84]

The big question now for a college to answer isn't "do we do online?" but rather "how much online?" Online course offerings are used to some extent by almost every college in the country, with many offering entire degree programs online. In many cases, the best way (at times the only way) to serve some market segments is through an online program. Other degree programs try to blend the best elements of online and place-based delivery. At large universities, it is very common for students to pick between online delivery and face-to-face delivery of the same course. In fact, many state universities make no distinction between online and face-to-face in undergraduate education. Take it whichever way you want, it shows up the same on your transcript.

But online is also relevant to small residential colleges. For quality purposes, they need to take an online (or a blended) approach to algorithm focused courses. Because of the structure of the subject matter, technology enhanced delivery of these types of courses is superior to pure face-to-face instruction. In other areas they might want to offer some online to give students a little more scheduling flexibility.

Online can also be quite helpful for courses that are severely undersubscribed. These are very common in senior level classes in small colleges. Total enrollment at small colleges is generally large enough to achieve course level economies of scale in lower division courses, but not at the upper division as students begin taking courses in different majors. This places the small college in severe cost disadvantage in offering these courses. This cost disadvantage can be overcome if the students of several small colleges can be combined into one online section.

## Excess Bricks and Mortar

It's not uncommon to see small private colleges struggling to meet payroll but at the same time engaged in a capital campaign to build a new science building and grow their endowment. These schools are operationally bankrupt but focused on becoming resource rich.

To many traditional college students and alumni (me included), nice buildings and grounds are important. While at some schools facilities may be over the top, the problem for most isn't that their buildings and land are too nice. Rather, it is that many of their buildings and land are not put to a productive use. Most colleges waste money on space that is little used.

Although they attract external criticism, the problem isn't with nice recreation facilities. Many students actually use them. Rather, it's with excess class rooms and oversized academic "temples"—science buildings and libraries. There are small teaching-focused colleges that have recently built elaborate science buildings that literally have more labs than they do science majors. Others have recently built large libraries to house hundreds of thousands of books.

Now nice science labs may be quite important to the education of science students, but does every science student need a lab of his/her own? Likely the capacity utilization rate of these labs is under 20%, yet they are a great source of pride to many college presidents.

Lots of students use libraries, but their function is to provide an appropriate ambience for study or daydreaming. They aren't of much importance to the undergraduate as a place to access books.

Library collections at teaching colleges were much bigger than they needed to be before the digitalization of knowledge. Now, they are just about pointless. It is rare that a student needs access to information that is not in their textbooks or available free on the Internet. When you add in reasonably priced access to proprietary databases, there isn't much need for an undergraduate library to have any books. In fact, from a need basis, you can't justify purchasing the number of books needed just to fill the shelves on the main reading room. The concept of stack space is a left-over artifact of the last millennium.

## Excess Endowment

Overall, it is understandable that the residential college education provided by most private non-profits requires them to make a much higher investment in land and building than do for-profits serving non-traditional segments. What doesn't make sense is the high level of financial assets that many non-profits own.

Except for the financial services industry, for-profit businesses rarely own a significant amount of financial assets. They maintain enough for working capital needs. Beyond that, financial assets are held short to medium term pending reinvestment in productive assets or return to shareholders. Yet most non-profit colleges have a significant amount of financial assets and are constantly striving to add more.

How can this behavior be explained? Henry Hansmann[85] of Yale Law School phrased this question as follows.

> The accumulation of endowment is, in effect, a form of saving, presumably for expenditure in the future. In a college or university, each dollar added to endowment represents a dollar less for current research or for educational services to current students or a dollar more in tuition that must be charged current students in order to provide them with the same level of services. The amounts thus saved will presumably be used to provide more research, more education, or lower tuition in the future. Why, then, do universities save rather than spend so much of their income?

Hansmann discusses a variety of reasons for this savings over spending behavior. One is to have a reserve against potential financial reversals resulting from revenue shortfalls or cost increases.

Compared to most businesses, college revenues are very stable. But colleges have more trouble cutting costs quickly in response to revenue declines. When you take in a student, you're making a multi-year commitment to provide services, and your biggest cost—faculty salaries—cannot be quickly adjusted downward to deal with revenue swings. In addition, colleges under financial duress have trouble borrowing (their assets are too organization-specific to make good collateral), and non-profit colleges do not have the legal ability to sell equity. So a good argument can be made that colleges should retain a higher level of savings than most businesses, but the actual level of savings at most colleges is much higher than is required for liquidity purposes.

Another reason for having an endowment is that major donations usually come in big lumps. The university can't rationally spend this money in the short-term, so the expenditures are spread out over several years. The smoother expenditure pattern provides a more efficient use of the donor's capital. This rational explains endowment savings for moderate time periods (say up to 20 years), but not perpetual endowments.

A reason for perpetual endowments is simply that's what the donor wants. Let's say a donor has $10,000 to give for a scholarship at a state university where in-state tuition is $10,000. That's enough to pay full tuition for one student for one year. However, the donor would rather provide a scholarship in perpetuity. So only $450 is available to be spent a year. This means the scholarship will pay tuition for only .045 students per year.

Regardless of whether donors' desires to achieve some immortality through their gifts is a good motive (it's certainly a desire that is impossible for a college to fulfill either physically or metaphysically), from the point of view of the college it is money they would not get otherwise. So, economically it makes sense to accept a donation in perpetuity even though the college would rather spend the money now.

Thus economically it might make sense for a college to have some endowment set aside for liquidity reasons, some for smoothing out expenditure of big donations, and some in perpetuity if the donor demands. Add the three together, and that should be the size of your endowment. However, it is clear that many college endowments now far exceed this amount; indeed most colleges have an explicit goal of increasing the size of their endowment. They love to raise "unrestricted" money and add to their quasi-endowment. (Legally they could spend the corpus, but they choose instead to treat the funds as under perpetual restrictions.)

As Hansmann points out, colleges rarely make any attempt to justify their super-saver behavior. When given, it focuses on the college providing equity between generations. Hansmann gives the following as an explicit description of this rationale.

> The trustees of an endowed institution are the guardians of the future against the claims of the present. Their task is to preserve equity among generations. The trustees of an endowed university ... assume the institution to be immortal. They want to know, therefore, the rate of consumption from endowment which can be sustained indefinitely.... In formal terms, the trustees are supposed to have a zero subjective rate of time preference.
>
> Consuming endowment income so defined means in principle that the existing endowment can continue to support the same set of activities that it is now supporting. This rule says that current consumption should not benefit from the prospects of future gifts to endowment. Sustainable consumption rises to encompass an enlarged scope of activities when, but not before, capital gifts enlarge the endowment.

In other words, the benefits of today's endowment should be shared equally between today's generation of students and future generation upon generation. This idea of intergenerational equity may sound noble of the current generation, but doesn't hold up under closer analysis. First, it only makes sense if you assume that future generations will be poorer than current generations. Why take from the poorer students of today to subsidize the richer students of 100 or 200 years from now? Or as Fred Flintstone might have asked, "why should Bedrock U give Peebles a skimpy scholarship in order to provide the same level of financial benefit to Judy Jetson?"

Second, even if you buy into the intergenerational equity concept as an ideal, it can't be done. It's hard enough to forecast revenue, gifts, and costs out for a few years; to think you can do it into perpetuity is to ascribe god-like foreknowledge to college administrators. In fact, as Hansmann demonstrates, it would be impossible to consistently provide intergenerational wealth equity even if all future revenues, gifts, and costs could be predicted.

Third, as Hansmann points out "transferring wealth from one generation to another is quite different from creating and disseminating knowledge, which is presumably the university's area of expertise...if a university wants to help future generations, financial investments may not be the best means to that end. Most university activities involve some sort of investment for the future. The research a university undertakes today, the education it provides, the faculty it builds, and the physical facilities it constructs will all yield a return for decades or even generations into the future. Accumulating funds in an endowment is worthwhile only if the return to endowment investments exceeds the returns from these other activities."[86]

While intergenerational equity is not a rational justification for big endowments, it does provide a good explanation for college behavior. Colleges today may be over-saving because the intergenerational equity argument sounds noble and they really haven't thought it through.

There are other explanations for the super-saver behavior that are not economically rational, but may be a good explanation of why it happens. Many university managers and faculty are extremely risk averse. To them, a large and growing endowment is a welcome sign of job security. Further, many are prone to believe that future uncertainty can be eliminated if one just plans enough today. So they plan excessively and often end up believing that their plan is indeed perfect.

Another reason that seems to be valid in many cases is that college presidents and trustees use it to show how successful their college is. Unlike the amount of learning occurring at a college, the size of endowment is easily observable and with good fund-raising and investing can grow significantly. So the size of the endowment is used as the sign of institutional success. More darkly, a huge endowment may stroke the ego of presidents, trustees, and alumni. As Hansman points out, it can become an unusual form of conspicuous consumption that he refers to as "conspicuous non-production ... since an endowment, in a sense, represents accumulated income that the university has been able to afford *not* to spend on education and research."

Now there is likely some truth to the managerial incompetence, managerial opportunism, and institutional ego explanations for large endowments; but it's hard to believe all trustees and college presidents are that incompetent, self-serving, and/or egotistical. Some certainly are, but thankfully many are not.

A likely reason for colleges' thirst for perpetual endowments is the simplest and most benign—early entrants in the industry did it (e.g., Oxford and Cambridge, then centuries later the American Ivies). At first, they gradually built up endowments for the rational reasons we have already mentioned. As endowments got excessive they likely didn't pay a whole lot of attention to the issue. Since these early colleges were extremely successful, other colleges started mimicking their behavior as much as possible without seriously examining why. Overtime the goal of having a big endowment became an industry norm that nobody in the industry ever questions.

Whatever the reason for big endowments, it is clear they are unproductive. A college should not devote time and resources trying to gain them. If a college has excess, then it should figure out how to put them to a productive use.

Let's take Saint John Doe College, a private religious school that targets a 1,500 student enrollment. Saint John Doe's annual costs (ignoring room and board) total $28 million. It has an endowment of $100 million. It takes $4 million a year out of the endowment to cover costs. Another $2 million a year comes from annual gifts. The remaining $22 (28-4-2) million comes from tuition. With 1,500 students, this means tuition of $14,667 a year. Now Saint John Doe is a good school but perennially struggles to attract enough students because its tuition is much higher than that of Big State U. In years when Saint John Doe doesn't get enough paying students, it has an operating deficit. While Saint John Doe College isn't a real school, the situation is quite real for many small schools.

Let's assume Saint John Doe doesn't change any of this in the future. We'll call this scenario "preserve the endowment." Alternatively, Saint John Doe's leadership could decide that building Saint John Doe's endowment doesn't really qualify as "storing up riches in heaven." They decide to set back $20 million of their endowment for liquidity purposes and spend the remaining $80 million over the next 20 years. This will generate over $6 million per year for the next 20 years. The $20 million liquidity portion of the endowment will generate $1 million a year, so $3 million needs to come out of the $6 million to keep tuition at the Preserve the Endowment level. This leaves Saint John Doe with an additional $3 million a year that it spends as scholarships to pay full tuition for 204 students. We'll call this scenario "education for this generation."

Certainly, Saint John Doe does a lot more good for 20 years under the "education for this generation" scenario. But what happens in 20 years when all the excess endowment is gone? The $20 million will still be in the endowment for liquidity purposes, but the scholarships will disappear. However, there never were any scholarships under the "preserve the endowment" scenario. Saint John Doe will be back to its current position as to scholarships. The $4 million that went from the endowment to support the general budget drops to $1 million, so tuition for students will have to go up from $14,667 to $16,667. So, during the next 20 years "educate this generation" provides over 1,000 people a free college education at the cost of a $2,667 tuition increase at the end of 20 years. And that's assuming nobody ever steps up in the next 20 years with more major donations.

|  | Preserve | This Gen | This Gen II |
|---|---|---|---|
| **Costs ($m)** | $28 | $28 | $28 |
| **Annual Donations ($m)** | 2 | 2 | 2 |
| **Endowment Earnings ($m)** | 4 | 1 | 1 |
| **Endowment Spend Down ($m)** |  | 3 |  |
| **Tuition Needed ($m)** | 22 | 22 | 25 |
| **Tuition per Student** | 14,667 | 14,667 | 16,667 |
| **Spend Down Scholarships ($m)** |  | 3 |  |

*People curse those who hoard grain, but they pray God's blessing on those who are willing to sell.*
Proverbs 11:26

Excessive endowments are an inefficient use of resources. But they are much worse than just an inefficiency. They can become destructive. Excess resources have a negative impact on any type of organization, and colleges are no exception to this rule. In fact, in the

*Wealth of Nations,* Adam Smith (a college professor) directly addresses the issue of college endowments.[87] He argues quite convincingly that an endowment allows institutions to become irrelevant (we get our money regardless of whether anybody wants to pay for what we do), faculty to become slothful (the money's the same no matter how badly I teach), administrators to proliferate (to manage the endowment and control slothful faculty), and all to adopt brother-in-law behavior (if you don't complain about my sloth and irrelevance, I won't complain about yours.)

Wealth allows a college to avoid taking actions that are clearly in the best interest of its students and society. Let's look at another scenario for Saint John Doe College. In the "education for this generation" scenario, Saint John Doe took the excess $80 million in endowment and spent it over 20 years. In our new scenario, rather than spending the excess endowment on scholarships, it converts it into 80 million one dollar bills, and then burns them in the Mother of All Homecoming bonfires. After the thrill of the bonfire is gone, Saint John Doe realizes that it must become Better/Cheaper in order to escape financial ruin. We'll call this the "bonfire of vanities" scenario.

Annual costs are now $15 million, a quite feasible number for a 1,500 student Better/Cheaper college. The $2 million dollars in annual gifts is still there, but only $1million is left annually from the endowment (remember the big bonfire). But since costs have been reduced, the amount of tuition revenue needed drops to $12 million, or $8,000 per student. This is a 43% drop in tuition from the "preserve the endowment" scenario and lets Saint John Doe go head-to-head with Big State U on tuition. Or if Saint John Doe wants to keep tuition at $14,667, it only needs 818 paying students. It could then provide a free education to 682 students a year for forever.

|  | Preserve | Bonfire |
| --- | --- | --- |
| **Costs ($m)** | $28 | $15 |
| **Annual Donations ($m)** | 2 | 2 |
| **Endowment Earnings ($m)** | 4 | 1 |
| **Tuition Needed ($m)** | 22 | 12 |
| **Tuition per Student** | $14,667 | $8,000 |

Now the bonfire scenario may be a little much. There are some better things you can do with your excess endowment than burn it. For example, Saint John could provide full-tuition scholarships to its entire student body for the next eight years, open partner colleges in Africa, or run an extensive missions program for its students and recent graduates. The point of the bonfire scenario is that excess endowment is bad for a college. Saint John Doe's management needs to heed the words of the Teacher.

> *I have seen a grievous evil under the sun:*
> *wealth hoarded to the harm of its owner.*
> Ecclesiastes 5:13

# 9

# Develop an Organizational Physiology that Fits

Taken individually, none of the ideas I've presented so far about how to design a college business model in order to achieve higher quality and lower cost are new. While the combination of all the ideas in the Better/Cheaper College model may be somewhat innovative, everything I've mentioned has been successfully put in practice somewhere in the United States. So why don't we have Better/Cheaper Colleges today? Much of the answer lies in the ownership problem discussed in Chapter 3. But the traditional nonprofit college's organizational physiology (its structure, systems/processes, and people) is also a major factor. To be a Better/Cheaper College, you must have an organizational physiology that fits being better and cheaper.

(Since some readers may be unfamiliar with the management concepts discussed in this chapter, I have included a generic explanation of each concept before giving specific applications for higher education. The generic explanations are printed in boxes. They come from *Strategic Innovation: New Game Strategies for Competitive Business Advantage*[88] by Allan Afuah, a professor at the University of Michigan.)

> Strategies are formulated and carried out by people; and people do differ. Moreover, the tasks that people must perform to execute a new game strategy vary from strategy to strategy. Therefore, not only do individuals need to perform different roles in the face of a new game strategy; what they need to motivate them to be effective at performing the tasks differs from task to task, from individual to individual, industry to industry, and country to country. Therefore, the type of people that a firm hires, who report to whom, how performance is measured and rewarded, and information systems needed, depend on the

type of new game strategy and environment in which the firm operates. Effectively, some organizational structures, systems/ processes and people would be more suitable for some strategies than others, given the environments in which the strategies must be executed. The objective in executing a new game strategy in a given environment is therefore to find those structures, systems, and people that best fit the set of activities that a firm chooses to perform, how, where, and when it performs them.

## Structure

While a firm's strategy is about the set of activities that the firm performs to create and appropriate value, a firm's structure tells us who reports to whom and who is responsible for which activities. An organizational structure has three primary goals. First, the structure of an organization should facilitate timely information flows to the right people for decision-making while preventing the wrong people from getting the information. Second, an effective structure requires the ability to be able to joggle ***differentiation (in the organizational structure sense)*** and integration. A firm's manufacturing and marketing units are maintained as separate functions because each one necessarily has to specialize in what it does in order to be both efficient and effective in carrying out its activities. Giving each unit the opportunity to specialize in what it does so as to be the best at it is what differentiation is about. However, to efficiently and effectively develop and offer customers unique benefits, a firm's different functions often have to interact across functions; that is, the value creation and appropriation activities of a firm's different functions must be ***integrated*** if it is going to perform well. Third, a final goal of an organizational structure is to coordinate interactions between units to effect integration. A new product launch would be more effective if the product development and marketing groups coordinated their activities—telling each other what they are doing, when and using information from each other as inputs.

## Develop an Organizational Physiology that Fits

To the casual observer, large research universities today resemble the big corporations of the 1970s: several big product/market silos (e.g., Arts & Sciences College, Business College, etc.) topped with a bloated corporate layer. On closer inspection, the problem is much worse. The product/market silos are actually composed of numerous smaller silos (academic departments) overlaid by the college's own corporate layer (the dean's office). The workers (faculty) reside within the departments and owe their organizational allegiance to their department. While housed within a college, the department owes it primary allegiance to its academic discipline (e.g., physics professors around the world) not the college in which they are housed, much less the university as a whole.

The result is lots of people working at cross purposes. Costs are high and quality is poor any time cooperation is required between colleges or departments. The president of one of the largest state research universities, Michael M. Crow of Arizona State University comments, "Our universities remain highly static, resistant to change, unwilling to evolve with real time, and focused primarily on their advancement of abstract knowledge... Organizational constraints derived from the flawed institutional design of our colleges and universities prevent them from realizing their entrepreneurial potential."[89]

Small teaching colleges look scarily like big research universities. Perhaps the corporate-level bloat is lower, but many still have product/market colleges with their own overhead. Even if they don't have this middle management tier, they still have lots of departments pursuing their own interests. And just like at big research universities, the departments owe their allegiance to their academic disciplines.

There is a better approach to structure. The key to success is to keep flat and group faculty by product/market. In a small teaching college, you just need one organizational level between president/provost and faculty, with these positions staffed part-time by faculty. As a college grows in size, another level will likely become necessary and the administrator full-time. But the key is never to create a grouping of employees based around an academic discipline.

Structuring a big research university is more complex because of its greater size and scope of operations. Many universities today retain a lot of power in the central level. This results in a highly bureaucratic decision-making process. In addition, the university level claims all the revenues the college produces and then determines what the colleges can spend. The result is that the profits the successful college makes are used to support unprofitable colleges and unnecessary corporate-level spending. This means that resources are raised based upon market needs but spent based upon internal politics. In other words, funding does not follow enrollment. This results in massive misallocation of resources.

A better approach that is used by some large universities is responsibility-centered management.[90] Here the goal is to decentralize decision-making by giving the college much more control. Basically, every college is a semi-autonomous profit center. This approach has helped improve the quality of decision-making, made colleges more cost conscious and more aggressive in seeking new revenues.

However, problems remain with resource allocation because at most universities central administration still retains control over a large percentage of revenues. At state schools, the norm is to let the college keep all tuition and other revenue they directly generate but to keep all state appropriations under central control. Central administration then distributes state appropriations based on "institutional priority," not student credit hours generated. In reality, "institutional priorities" translates into supporting unprofitable programs and unnecessary corporate level spending—the very same problems the purely centralized traditional approach has. To improve resource allocation, the amount of revenue that central administration controls needs to be substantially decreased from current levels.

Over time, universities should move to a structure where the individual units (academic colleges and research institutes) are largely autonomous of each other, cooperating under a confederation-type government.[91] A few things should be done in common, like intercollegiate athletics, physical campus planning, and the university calendar; but most operations (and necessary decision-making power and financial resources) are at the unit level.

As with the small college, the big university has disciplinary departments, but there are more of them and they are larger in size. Disciplinary departments cause big universities the same problems they do small colleges. However, they may be unavoidable because most research and many graduate programs are discipline-based.

Perhaps the best solution is to group faculty members by 1) product/market for teaching and research, and 2) in a formal network by academic discipline. Faculty would be in one product/market unit for their teaching and another for their research. This would not be a matrix structure where faculty would have one job and two bosses, but rather a structure with two jobs and two bosses. While more confusing and costly than the classic one job/one boss approach, it does recognize that faculty in a research school have two very different jobs—teaching and research. Our current approach gives faculty two jobs and one boss, and that boss consistently emphasizes research at the expense of teaching.

To aid voluntary cooperation and collaboration between faculty with similar interests, formal faculty networks would be established for academic disciplines. These disciplinary networks might have a faculty member serving as part-time administrator of the network, but this faculty member would not have any managerial power over the faculty in the network. Further, the disciplinary network would not have any formal role in any decision-making process.[92]

## Systems/Processes

> Organizational structures are about who reports to whom and what activities they perform, but say very little about how to keep employees motivated as they carry out their assigned tasks and responsibilities in executing a strategy. *Systems* are about the incentives, performance requirements and measures, and information flow and accountability mechanisms that facilitate the efficient and effective execution of strategies.
>
> ***Organizational systems*** are about how the performance of individuals, groups, functional units, divisions, and organizations is sought, monitored, measured, and compensated. They include financial measures such as profits, market share, cash flows, gross profit margins, stock market price, return on investment, earnings per share, return on equity, and economic value added (EVA). Organizational systems also include reward systems such as pay scales, profit-sharing, employee stock option plans (ESOPs), bonuses, and nonfinancial rewards such as recognition with certificates or having one's name engraved somewhere on a product that

> one helped develop. Systems also include so-called processes. A firm's ***processes*** are the "patterns of interaction, coordination, communication, and decision making [that] employees use to transform resources into products and services of greater worth." These patterns of communication, interaction, coordination, and decision-making are a function of the type of strategy, organizational structure, and incentive system in place.

While there are several systems/processes at colleges, let's focus on the two that are the traditional whipping boys—tenure and decision-making.

**Tenure.** Tenure has been the subject of much analysis. George Leef of the John William Pope Center for Higher Education Policy provides an excellent summary

> People usually think that tenure ensures guaranteed lifetime employment, but that isn't exactly correct. As Professors Roger Meiners and Ryan Amacher point out in their book *Faulty Towers: Tenure and the Structure of Higher Education*, a tenured faculty member is legally entitled to a set of legal safeguards that the institution must overcome before it can terminate his employment. Untenured faculty members, on the other hand, can be dismissed like any other employee.
>
> Because the hurdles are so difficult in proving good cause to terminate a tenured professor, schools usually leave them alone. The University of Colorado's decision to fire the infamous "Ethnic Studies" professor Ward Churchill for plagiarism and academic fraud led to difficulties barely less onerous than landing a man on the moon. Only in the rare and egregious case will a school decide to go to the trouble. [A more common, but still rare, occurrence is when faculty are terminated because of financial distress at their college (Tulane did this after Hurricane Katrina) or because the program the faculty was affiliated with was eliminated (this occasionally happens to departments with minimal internal political power.)]
>
> The justification invariably given for tenure is that it is needed to protect professorial freedom—to speak and write freely. Otherwise, it's argued hostile administrators or

trustees could easily fire professors for saying things they didn't like. That did happen on occasion early in the 20th century and there was reason to protect faculty members against autocratic overseers.

But as history professor Page Smith writes in his book *Killing the Spirit*, "What faculty needed and deserved to have was review procedures that protected them from arbitrary actions by administrators or trustees. What they got was much more: a degree of security unequaled by any other profession and difficult to justify in abstract terms."[93]

While legally tenure isn't total job security, in practice it is. There is concern that people will work less after they get tenure. From 23 years on faculty (16 with tenure), I haven't noticed many faculty working less once they are tenured. However, there is a big problem when people are tenured who shouldn't have been. The college is stuck with them for life.

Due to tenure, the college cannot replace them with better performing faculty. This harms the productivity of the college. This is a huge problem in the humanities where tenure is used by current faculty to protect their jobs at the expense of the new entrant who would be willingly to do better work at lower pay.

Tenure also reinforces ITC ownership of the college. In order to achieve tenure, one must be approved by the existing members of the ITC. Once tenured, you have lifetime membership in the ITC. Financially, the salaries of tenured faculty have first claim on the revenues of the college. If the tenured faculty aren't major owners of most colleges, who is?

As Leef concludes:

> Tenure goes well beyond what was (and perhaps still is) needed to shield faculty members against unjust dismissal. All that is needed is a "just cause" clause in the employment contract stating that the faculty member may only be fired for certain kinds of conduct, which do not include speaking freely. Institutions could customize the language to suit their situations. Schools with a religious mission might wish to restrict faculty free speech that questioned the tenets of their religion. The legitimate objective of protection against arbitrary dismissal can be achieved through contract.

Tenure was never a very good idea, and in this time when most colleges and universities need to find ways to get the most educational value for their (now lessened) money, it shouldn't be treated like a sacred cow.[94]

***Decision-making.*** University decision-making processes have also been a subject of study. In fact, the well known "garbage can" model of organizational decision-making achieved prominence in 1974 based on a study of college decision-making by James March and Herb Simon.[95]

College decision-making suffers on multiple fronts. A quick decision is one that is made in a year (literally). Most administrators and faculty are risk averse, so analysis paralysis prevails. Colleges should heed the advice of Collins and Lazier.

> Analysis allows us to say "maybe," but life ... does not. Judicious use of analysis is good as long as you don't fall prey to "analysis paralysis." There are seldom enough facts or data to eliminate all risk or to make a decision based solely on those facts...Facts, analyses, and probabilities all have their place in decision making. Just remember that the objective is to *make a decision*, not to pulverize it with analysis.[96]

Slow decisions aren't the only problem. Many faculty want to be very involved in decision-making, even though the question to be decided is totally outside of their area of responsibility or expertise. There is an emphasis on reaching a decision by consensus. This is generally very difficult, if not impossible, since the interests of administrators and faculty are often in conflict. Even more significantly the interests of different groups of faculty are rarely the same. The result is a highly politicized suboptimal decision. Actually suboptimal is a kind evaluation of many decisions. As one can see from the general education requirements at many schools, horrible is a better word to describe the outcome of much college decision-making. Yet these horrible decisions are implemented, often to the personal benefit of those who made them. As Thomas Sowell points out:

> Among the leading institutional liabilities of American colleges and universities are tenure and faculty self-governance. While tenure in the academic world is not as destructive of incentives as it is in the public schools, because academic tenure is not combined with lock-step pay and

promotion based on the mere passage of time, academic tenure is made more pernicious than it needs to be by being combined with faculty self-governance and the up-or-out system of promotion. The temptation of log-rolling is very strong among colleagues who must regard each other as "facts of life" for years to come. More fundamentally, it is the wholly unaccountable nature of faculty self-governance which makes it so dangerous—and so vulnerable to strident groups, threatening to make life unpleasant on campus for all who oppose their demands.

While the faculty as a whole will suffer if their decisions drive the college or university into financial straits, that is a very weak incentive or constraint for an individual faculty member pushing an individual project. This is one of the inherent problems of collectivized decision-making by unaccountable individuals, whether in an academic setting or a political setting, here or overseas. Yet seldom, if ever, is collectivized decision-making so utterly unaccountable as among college and university professors.

Elected officials in democratic countries can be defeated for re-election or even recalled during their terms of office. In totalitarian countries, they are purged. Among business decision-makers, red ink can destroy even the biggest corporations in a relatively short time if the situation is not turned around, and even a failure to make the most of profit opportunities can attract hostile takeover bids or a stockholder revolt that ends in heads rolling in the executive suites. Yet absolutely nothing prevents a tenured professor from promoting or voting for disastrous institutional policies for years—or decades—on end.

It would be considered a gross violation of "academic freedom" to fire anyone because the policies he supported in faculty meetings over the years have led to a drastic decline in the college or university's academic standing or financial viability. In virtually no other institution anywhere is there such a blank check for irresponsibility.[97]

So, for a variety of reasons, current college decision-making processes are wasteful and often result in poor decisions from the perspective of the institution and its students. Tremendous improvements could be made in institutional performance by: 1) setting reasonable time limits to make a decision, 2) more use of participative decision making (input is sought from various people, but one person actually makes the decision) rather than consensual, and 3) holding people accountable for the results of their decisions.

## People

> People are central to any strategy since they conceive of, formulate, and execute strategies. The extent to which a firm's employees can thrive within its organizational structure, are motivated by the performance and reward systems that it has put in place, or effectively use the information systems that it established, is a function of the firm's organizational culture, resources, and capabilities and the types of employee.

***Resources and capabilities.*** No matter what the industry, a portion of a firm's resources and capabilities resides in the people within the firm. This is particularly true in professional service firms like law firms, consulting firms, and colleges. The bulk of what a college does is to unite professionals in the direct provision of services to students and society. The quality of the end product is highly dependent upon the professionals and how they interact.

> ***Types of People***—Quite simply, not everyone is meant for every job. Nor is every reward system going to motivate every employee. Thus, in executing a strategy, it is important to get the right people to perform the right tasks.

David Maister's matrix of types of professional work offers insight into the types of people colleges need.[98] When applying Maister's matrix to higher education, "the instructional side of faculty work is primarily nursing with a little bit of psychotherapy mixed in. The research side of faculty work is brain surgery." When hiring faculty to teach, you want to hire people who are excellent nurses, not brain surgeons. Some faculty can do both well, but many can't. A school should not have someone doing nursing work who is not a good nurse. Unfortunately, research-oriented schools regularly hire for skills as a brain surgeon and not a nurse. Many faculty are not very interested in teaching, particularly undergraduate teaching.

| Maister's Matrix of Professional Work | | |
|---|---|---|
| | **STANDARDIZED PROCESS** Emphasis on Execution | **CUSTOMIZED PROCESS** Emphasis on Diagnosis |
| **HIGH CLIENT CONTACT** Value Added in Front Room | NURSE | PSYCHOTHERAPIST |
| **LOW CLIENT CONTACT** Value Added in Back Room | PHARMACIST | BRAIN SURGEON |

On top of that, basic teaching and communications skills may be lacking.

To teach, faculty need to be knowledgeable about their fields. However, this does not require that they be good researchers. In fact, it is quite possible to be a successful researcher yet not know much that students need to learn. Academic research prowess isn't the same as broad knowledge about a field and the wisdom to apply that knowledge to real world problems.

The academic world traditionally attaches much more prestige and pay to brain surgery. Most faculty want to be Brain Surgeons even though most are not very good at it. On top of that, many faculty want to be managed as if they were doing brain surgery even when they are doing nursing. This doesn't work well because the nature of the work is very different. Brain surgery is custom work and performed largely independent of the other professionals in a college. Nursing is relatively standardized work and performed interdependently with other professionals. Nurse processes need to be standardized and performed in a consistent manner. If not, quality slips and costs go up.

**Faculty values.** If a college is serious about a set of values, it needs to hire faculty who have those values and live by them. Except for some religious colleges, this certainly isn't the case today. Harry Lewis presents this point strongly in recounting his experiences as dean of Harvard College. "If we really want closer student-faculty contact, if we really expect faculty to guide student's lives and not just their studies, then we owe it to students and their families to appoint professors with whom we would want our own children to have close personal contact."⁹⁹

You also want faculty who are not totally financially driven. Yes, you have to pay competitive salaries with other colleges to get good faculty. But you do not have to pay them as much as they could earn in a "real job." There are many nonfinancial benefits of being college faculty. Scheduling and time demands are such that one can have a great lifestyle outside of work (you can make it to the kid's school programs, you're never on weekend call, you don't have to check in daily while on vacation, you can get paid to spend a month in Europe touring around). In addition, you get paid for satisfying your intellectual curiosity or being involved in public service. Most importantly, working with college students can be enjoyable and rewarding.

Lots of people are quite willing to make some financial trade-offs to be a college professor. While their "real world" earnings potential is relevant to what you have to pay to get good faculty (that's why you have to pay business professors a lot more than liberal arts professors), you don't have to match it. In fact, you do not want people who expect you to match it. You want people who value the nonfinancial rewards the job provides.

## Culture

> A firm's culture is critical to its ability to create and appropriate value. Basically, people within an organizational structure and associated systems develop shared values (what is important) and beliefs (how things work). These shared values and beliefs then influence who else is hired or stays in the organization, how it is reorganized and how the systems change or do not change. The results of these interactions are behavioral norms (the way we do things), which then determine how well a strategy is implemented or formulated. If the structure, systems, and people are just right, the norms can lead to a system of activities that is difficult to imitate. If is not right, culture can be a competitive disadvantage.

The right culture for a Better/Cheaper College may vary from college to college, but it must be a culture that encourages its people to behave as professionals. A **profession** is a vocation founded upon specialized educational training, the purpose of which is to supply disinterested counsel and service to others.[100] Unfortunately, as I have already discussed at length, the dominant culture in higher education is the Ivory Tower. The Ivory Tower acts in its own best interests, rather than the best interests of the students and society it is supposed to be serving. A college cannot deliver high quality and low cost and have an Ivory Tower culture.

# Part IV

# Conclusion

## *Making Better/Cheaper a Reality*

**Chapter 10: Take Action**

# 10

# Take Action

In this last part of the book, let's turn attention to making Better/Cheaper a reality. On the one hand, as discussed in Part II, a college can become Better/Cheaper immediately by adopting an innovative business model. On the other hand, as discussed in Part I, there are major barriers to strategic innovation inside today's colleges. What can be done now?

As the subtitle of the book suggests, the answer is be entrepreneurial. Being entrepreneurial doesn't just mean designing innovative business models. It also means taking an entrepreneurial approach to the spread of innovation through the higher education industry. It does not mean trying to pursue a top-down, national industrial policy for higher education. Rather, entrepreneurs should come forward today with Better/Cheaper Colleges and then the rest of industry will incrementally change in response. You can't expect the industry to change overnight, but it will not begin to change until entrepreneurs take action. Where should we look for entrepreneurial action today, and what can be done to support it?

## Small Private Colleges

Better/Cheaper models should be particularly appealing to most small private undergraduate colleges. Although most are currently profitable, they are strategically bankrupt. The model they are following works great for the rich private college serving the prestige segment, but most small private colleges do not have the immense wealth and brand name of a high prestige college. Their current model is not economically sustainable for them.

Converting to a Better/Cheaper College is necessary for these colleges' long-term economic stability. A Better/Cheaper model makes them a vastly better value than competing private colleges. Perhaps more importantly, Better/Cheaper allows them to be price competitive with public colleges. With price competitiveness, a private college can compete in the value market by offering its target market more benefits than the state college, e.g., quality liberal education, small school feel, chance to participate in intercollegiate athletics, religious programming, etc. Better/Cheaper models should be particularly attractive to private colleges with a strong commitment to transmitting moral values to the next generation. By being cost-competitive, they can increase enrollment, hence expanding the number of students who are exposed to the college's values.

Despite these obvious advantages, most private colleges will not be interested. You can't become a Better/Cheaper College without changing ownership. The problem isn't that we don't know how to be Better/Cheaper, it is that the ITC owns the college. Cutting costs means eliminating ITC profits. The major way to reduce profits is to reduce administrator/faculty headcount. Colleges are unwilling to do this. Rather than reduce headcount in order to reduce price, they raise price in order to increase headcount.

Most private colleges refer to their governing board as a Board of Trustees. As trustees, they are legally charged with making decisions that are in the best interests of their beneficial owners. The problem with most trustees is that they make decisions in the best interests of the ITC. Decisions are made to maximize ITC profits. Sometimes trustees may be called upon to resolve conflicts between competing insider groups, but actions are never intentionally taken that would result in an overall reduction of ITC profit.

In order to improve quality and reduce costs, trustees must view their beneficial owners as students, parents, and society. Trustees must act in the best interests of their students. Certainly you need to deal fairly with your employees, but they are just that, employees. They do not own the college. The purpose of the college is to provide an education to its students, not to provide pleasant employment for faculty and administrators. Once a board of trustees fully commits to serving the best interests of students, then the path to doing so is straightforward and relatively quick for a small private college.

The key is to have a good president and back him to the fullest. The small college is like a medium-sized business. The president can't micro-manage but can be very aware of what is happening and directly involved in all major decisions. Literally, the president can know every employee and personally approve all invoices. As a result, a president of a small college can quickly and effectively make major changes.

The president must both understand how to run a college and want to run it for the benefit of the students, not the ITC. Unfortunately, this does not describe most college presidents. Presidents that came up from within academe are deeply steeped in the existing management practices of higher education. They rose to power by being successful working within the current system, not challenging it. They do not see that there is a better way. Most are true believers in the Ivory Tower. They are opposed to the Better/Cheaper College. Even if not a true believer in the Ivory Tower, they rose to the top by not challenging its ways.

A president from outside academe isn't necessarily the answer. They are heavily handicapped by not understanding the day-to-day operational side of college. As a result, they are reluctant to push major change. Further, many are attracted to the presidency as a more pleasant job than a private sector position. They aren't coming to academe to reform an industry.

However, getting a good president isn't a hopeless task. You are just unlikely to find one through the normal search process, which is designed to find a president that is popular with the education establishment. The Better/Cheaper College is anathema to the education establishment.

Major cost savings and tuition cuts can be achieved in two years or less. As high as costs currently are, it is easy to identify major ways to cut costs. As we have already discussed, there is a lot of room for cost savings in many parts of the college. However, the quickest route to major cost savings is to reduce faculty headcount by the elimination or consolidation of low enrollment majors.

The first step in the process is to compute the net revenue per program. This is a relatively straightforward calculation. Revenue is the student credit hours generated by the program multiplied by net tuition per student credit hour (plus state subsidy for public colleges) plus grant and endowment income specific to that program. This revenue number is then netted against the programs variable costs (mostly faculty salaries).

After the net revenue per program is determined, you then need to charge the program with all your other costs that cannot be directly charged to specific programs. This is done on a per-student basis. The result is a net/net revenue per program.

Your various academic programs will fall into one of three groups. First are the ones that are positive on a net/net basis. These are clearly good programs and should be kept. The second are those that are negative on a net/net basis but positive on a net basis. These programs cover all of their direct instructional costs and produce some cash that can be used to pay noninstructional costs. However, they are not paying their full share of noninstructional costs. Deciding what to do with these programs requires a more involved analysis on both a qualitative and quantitative basis. Some should stay, but some may need to go.

The final group is made up of programs that have negative net revenue. A program that is generating negative net revenue isn't making any contribution to covering noninstructional costs. In fact, it is being subsidized by the positive net revenue programs. Negative net revenue programs should be eliminated or consolidated into programs that can at least generate net revenues.

This will, of course, be opposed by faculty whose jobs are eliminated. Who can blame them? However, the issue for the school is whose financial interests come first—those of the current faculty or the students? Some will object that "we can't call ourselves a university and not have physics major (or philosophy or German, etc.)." This argument appeals to the Ivory Tower. Students don't care.

These programs drive up cost without adding any value, except for the very few students who want to major in them. Not having a full program in a discipline does not mean that you aren't teaching courses in that discipline. For example if you offer only two physics courses, you will be meeting the needs of almost all students who are science majors; or you can require a Philosophies of Life course as part of general education without having a philosophy major.

In addition, realize that achieving positive net revenue is a very low bar for a program to chin. You are not requiring the program make a profit, only that it recover its direct costs. With noninstructional costs at most colleges about half of total costs, a program that doesn't even recoup its direct instructional costs is an extremely weak program. Yet most non-profits are unwilling even to eliminate these obviously weak programs.

The issue today isn't figuring out how to cut costs, rather it is actually doing it. Adopting a profits-to-the-students approach is possible; however, it requires a committed president and a board of trustees to wage the inevitable fight with the ITC.

## Multi-College University

At the other end of the spectrum from the small, private college is the big, multi-college research university. It is a large, diversified, and complex organization. A quick conversion of the entire university to Better/Cheaper is probably impossible. However, a semi-autonomous Better/Cheaper College could be created today as just one of the many colleges in a multi-college university. This would allow the university to pursue innovation through a new Better/Cheaper College without disrupting their existing colleges' activities. Because the new college would be operationally self-sufficient, it can provide its value proposition without interfering with the operations of the rest of the university. In fact, the Better/Cheaper College would need little from the university. The major benefit to undergraduate students from being at a big university is not in the classroom but rather in the overall, big school environment. This is achieved simply by being physically located at a big university and having access to university-wide student life (student organizations, speakers, intramurals, intercollegiate athletics, community social life, etc.).

These Better/Cheaper Colleges within the university would focus their efforts on undergraduate instruction. They would also provide a much smaller community for the student within the bigger community. In effect, students would have the best of both worlds: the personal attention and undergraduate focus of the small private college, and the diversity and activity of the large university.

This approach would also allow public colleges to provide a solid liberal education. Currently, liberal education is a conundrum for public universities. They are tasked with serving a broad spectrum of society with diverse views. This diversity does not pose a problem when dealing with scholarship and education in technical areas. (Flipping the switch completes the circuit and turns on the lights for both the Secular Progressive and Traditional Christian). However, regularly in the humanities, and often the social sciences, it doesn't work that way. The particular view one takes matters a lot.

For example, a movement called Spirituality in Education is currently popular among some in public education circles. It argues "for educating the whole student without indoctrination and through the enhancement of existing academic values and programs."[101] A main tenant for many in the movement is "religion is not about accepting 20 impossible propositions before breakfast, but about doing things that change you. It is a moral aesthetic, an ethical alchemy. The myths and laws of religion are not true because they conform to some metaphysical, scientific, or historical reality but because they are life enhancing."[102] That may be a great tenant for a liberal education for Spiritualists, but it certainly would be a liberal education widely at odds to Christian belief.

Public universities can try to avoid this pluralism-of-views problem by taking a universal approach that provides a neutral overview of multiple perspectives. In practice, this is difficult to pull off because it requires a very tight control of faculty teaching potentially controversial courses. Left unchecked, many faculty promote their own particular views, and more problematically attack students with opposing views.

Even if the public university can pull off this neutral approach, it results in a very weak form of liberal education. Public universities can do a lot things well (research, public service, science instruction, professional education), but liberal education isn't one of them. So how can a public university deal with liberal education?

A viable solution is to take a minimalist approach within the public university but provide students with the opportunity to have a more particular, richer liberal education by cooperating with private residential colleges operating under a Better/Cheaper model. Students desiring a more robust liberal education could enroll in the participating residential college of their choice. These residential colleges would be privately operated and take any approach to liberal education that they saw fit. These residential colleges would provide residential life, the for-credit academic courses to "know right," and other programs to "do right." They could take a broad approach or a very particular approach. They could be like Bob Jones University, or the Spiritualist, or whatever. The key is that students are free to pick among them, and are not required to participate at all.

While Better/Cheaper Colleges within a multi-college university would be highly beneficial to students, there are major barriers to implementation of this approach. In addition to the barriers to liberal education in general discussed in Chapter 4, there are organizational barriers. Administrators are reluctant to give up power and resources to organizations they do not control. They also have a general inclination to view uniformity as better than plurality. In addition to administrator opposition, faculty in the humanities and social sciences will be strongly opposed since this approach would lead to a significant loss of their current intellectual authority and money to the residential colleges. ITC profits would be transferred from them to the students.

## For Profits

In recent decades, for-profit colleges have driven innovation in the higher education industry. They started by serving the unserved nontraditional student market and then led the way to online. Because they are not subject to the constraints of ITC ownership, their cost structure is such that they are in a position to deliver the cheaper part of better/cheaper. However, for-profits have historically avoided competing on price.

While not as eye-popping as the non-profits' margins, most for-profits have very good profit margins with growing enrollments. Why should they reduce their price? One reason is to increase market share. In fact, in some states public college tuition is so high that a for-profit could price compete with the state regional colleges for the commuter student market. But why lower price when in many states like California the state regional colleges are driving students to you already by limiting enrollments to protect their own profit margins?

Lower prices may not make sense today from a pure economic standpoint, but owners of for-profit businesses have the right to forego profits if they so desire. If the founders don't need outside capital, then the founders can do as they please. If outside capital is necessary, there may be social investors willing to take a lower financial return to support education. Or under current financial market conditions, some financially-oriented investors might be delighted to have a stable preferred dividend with some inflation protection. A for-profit social entrepreneurial approach may not be a path to an IPO, but the amount of capital needed isn't that much. Non-bricks and mortar colleges do not need large amounts of capital unless they are making acquisitions. The capital needs of many for-profits are low enough that they do not need to be public companies.

## For Profit Managers/Non-Profit Owners

In fact, from an overall industry perspective, the issue isn't how to get more capital into the industry but how to properly utilize existing capital. Most non-profits, both state-owned and private, are well capitalized but underperforming. One way to deal with this problem is for the non-profit college to partner with a for-profit. The idea is to partner the capital of the non-profit with the expertise and business discipline of the for-profit for the overall benefit of the non-profit's students.

For example, a local non-profit college might enter into a joint venture with a national for-profit management company. The national for-profit would provide day-to-day management of the local non-profit college. The local college chooses what programs it wants to offer, their level of difficulty, and what values will be taught. The for-profit then provides all necessary services for a set charge per student. Profits and losses belong to the non-profit.

Since the non-profit is providing all the buildings, the capital needs of the for-profit national management company would be low enough that it could actually be owned by its faculty, in the same way that law firms, accounting firms, and many consulting firms are owned by their partners. As a professional services firm, the management company would staff the college with faculty and staff acceptable to the college's trustees. Several of the faculty and senior administrators of the partner college would be partners in the professional services firm. The professional services firm would charge enough to cover costs and earn a profit for its partners.

Competitive forces will keep the professional services firm's price down and quality up. If either flags, the local college has the option of switching to another partner. Tuition should be much lower to the student. The local college has negotiated a favorable price with its partner so cost of instruction is lower. The non-profit local college is likely to pass these savings on to its students since the actual cost of operations is transparent to the trustees.

## State Government

The following table is a list of in-state tuition at several state-owned Big Research Universities. Given that tuition in about every state is $8,000 or above, in-state undergraduate students are currently

## In-State Tuition & Fees, Public Research Universities 1980 and 2010

| University | 2010 In-State Tuition & Fees[103] | 1980 In-State Tuition & Fees (2010$) |
|---|---|---|
| Pennsylvania State University | $17,344 | $4,272 |
| University of Illinois-Urbana Champaign | $15,144 | $2,561 |
| University of Michigan-Ann Arbor | $14,168 | $3,822 |
| University of California-Berkeley | $12,461 | $1,994 |
| University of Colorado at Boulder | $11,960 | $2,590 |
| University of Kansas | $11,780 | $2,007 |
| University of Virginia-Main Campus | $10,906 | $2,712 |
| University of Connecticut | $10,416 | $2,780 |
| University of Kentucky | $9,813 | $1,775 |
| Texas A & M University | $9,606 | $1,273 |
| University of Iowa | $9,220 | $2,160 |
| The University of Texas at Austin | $8,930 | $1,176 |
| Ohio State University-Main Campus | $8,679 | $2,890 |
| Indiana University-Bloomington | $8,613 | $2,637 |
| University of Wisconsin-Madison | $8,310 | $2,619 |
| University of California- Los Angeles | $8,266 | $1,976 |
| University of Maryland-College Park | $8,053 | $2,301 |
| University of Alabama | $7,900 | $1,991 |
| University of North Carolina-Chapel Hill | $6,666 | $1,556 |
| University of Florida | $5,381 | $1,931 |

Source: University Web pages, National Center for Education Statistics, Author's Calculations

paying the full cost of their education, some much more than that. Yet these schools are heavily subsidized by the state. In fact, in most states, higher education takes up 15 to 20% of total state appropriations. That's a lot of money. Where does it go?

At Big Research U, some of it goes for research and public service. Whether this is a good expenditure of tax dollars is not the subject of my analysis, so I'll just take it as a given. However, most of the state subsidy is not designated for research and public service, even at Big Research U. It is supposed to be subsidizing undergraduate education for state residents. But what is happening now is that the subsidy is ITC profit that the college gets to spend on things that are not necessary to provide a quality undergraduate education.

This wasn't how state-owned colleges and universities originally operated. The second column of Table 1 shows 1980 in-state tuition stated in 2010 dollars. As you can see, as late as 30 years ago the subsidy provided major benefits to state residents. State colleges and universities have used the wild run-up in prices over recent decades to drastically raise their profits. Students now pay the full cost of their education, with the state funds now going to ITC profits.

State taxpayers certainly have a right to feel exploited. However as a long-time faculty member at a state-owned Big Research U, let me say a few things in our defense. First, from a faculty perspective, we are not in a position to control overall costs. In fact, we work in an organization that gives us strong incentives to maximize spending. Our administrators have certainly been aggressively gobbling up every dollar in sight—whether from student or state. Yet I think most of these administrators had good intentions. I don't think most set out to deliberately drive up tuition. Further, since most are firm believers in the Ivory Tower, they see nothing wrong in taking vastly more money from students. What better thing to do than to make more profit that can be spent for the glory of the Ivory Tower?

State governments have also played a huge role in causing the problem. They have encouraged us to compete in the reputation market. Further, they often view colleges as job-creating pork for their districts. They force individual state college and universities to work through a central bureaucracy that makes rules that drive up costs and is often publicly committed to raising costs. (We are actually encouraged to bring spending up to be in line with our peers!) While some of these actions are taken for strictly political gain, most are well-intentioned.

Trying to fix the high cost problem overnight without massive disruption to the system is impossible. The existing business model of state colleges and universities needs to be radically changed. These changes have to happen at the individual school level. You can't intelligently mandate what each school needs to do. Centralized decision-making to achieve local-level innovation is impossible.

Successful innovation requires local knowledge and local action.[104] The best course of action varies from one locality to another. Much of the most important knowledge is tacit. That means the knowledge is personal to the holder and is hard, if not impossible, for the holder to explicitly communicate to another person. As a result, most viable opportunities for innovation are recognized and/or created at the local level. Successful innovation also requires action at the local level. While a governmental educational authority may be able to regulate bad behavior it cannot mandate good behavior.[105] Regulation certainly cannot mandate innovation. Instead the state should use market mechanisms to promote innovation.

**Defund higher education?** The state higher education problem is magnified in states that are currently in a financial crisis mode. Since all the state subsidy is going to ITC profits, from a taxpayer standpoint the subsidy is a prime example of government waste. So why not just eliminate the subsidy, set the individual colleges free from central regulation, and let the chips fall where they may? This will have a huge positive impact on a state's budget but would be very chaotic for existing students in the short-term. In addition, the move would likely be very politically unpopular in the short run as public colleges would react by trying to raise tuition and/or limit access. The public colleges can also correctly argue that they are not the cause of the huge growth in state spending. (Remember, state support in real dollars has remained constant, not grown, as state budgets have mushroomed). However, the financial situation in some states is dire, and higher education may be viewed as one of the best places to make major cuts. The issue in these states will be how to make major cuts quickly in a manner that causes the least harm to current students.

Let's turn to states in a more solid financial position. They need things to change, but change can occur at a more gradual pace. Their problem isn't that they can't financially support higher education at the current level; it's that their support is not being used well. What should they do?[106] There are two basic problems with the way that state funded higher education is designed. First, state-owned schools operate as a cartel. Second, state funding only goes to state-owned schools.

**Break up the public school cartel.** In most states, state-owned colleges are given distinct geographic territories (Southeastern XYZ State College can't open up a branch outside of the southeast part of the state) and market verticals (XYZ State University can't open a medical school because that is a protected vertical for the University of XYZ). The justification given for the cartel is to "keep costs down by avoiding unnecessary duplication of programs." This is the standard justification offered by cartels in the private sector. This is a much more socially acceptable justification than the real reason. What a cartel is really saying is "No duplicate programs means no competition. No competition means higher profits for cartel member at the expense of the consumer." In the private sector, U.S. law makes cartels illegal, even criminal at times. However, cartels are legally sanctioned in state higher education. In fact, in many states the individual institutions are required to charge students a set cartel price.

States would get much more bang for their buck if they broke up the cartel and let state-owned colleges compete with each other. From a technical standpoint, this would be a somewhat complex legal undertaking whose details would vary from state to state. But the basics steps are pretty simple. Tie the state subsidy directly to enrollment, let the schools offer any program they want at any place they want, and let them cut prices to pick up students from other state colleges. By increasing choice and competition, over time public schools will be forced to increase their quality and lower their price.

While technically quite doable, breaking up the cartel may prove very difficult politically. The current cartel arrangement provides major financial benefits to its members, many of whom are politically powerful. Given the large numbers of state institutions, it is almost certain that some would not survive in a competitive market. While competitively weak, they still have some political muscle. A bigger problem is that while the strong schools will gain market share, their ITC profits are likely to drop as overall industry profitability will drop due to lower prices. Since the political power of the state research universities and bigger regional colleges is significant, breaking up the cartel will be politically challenging. In addition, switching from a bureaucratic to an entrepreneurial mindset will be very difficult for state governments.

A quick break-up of the cartel is unlikely. However, to demonstrate the power of Better/Cheaper College, a state governing body might create a new (or convert an old) college as a Better/Cheaper College and allow it to operate on a small scale free of the anti-competitive constraints of the cartel. As the pilot is successful, over time other colleges will imitate it—both because the pilot has demonstrated the benefits of Better/Cheaper and because the pilot's success will put competitive and political pressure on underperforming institutions to change.

***Create private charter colleges.*** A bigger problem than the cartel is that by state law the state subsidy is only paid to state-owned colleges. This gives them a huge competitive advantage over private colleges. State colleges can spend just as much as a private college but then charge a substantially lower price due to the subsidy. The subsidy makes it hard for private colleges to compete in the huge value segment.

The good news is that this subsidy can be dealt with legislatively without the need for cooperation from state-owned colleges. This can be done by using the state subsidy to develop partnerships with private colleges to improve value. At their option, private colleges located within the state could become private charter colleges. These private charter colleges would enter into a partnership arrangement with the state. In return for the state subsidy, the private college would agree to charge in-state students the same price, or lower, than the public colleges currently do.

Let's look at a fairly typical, mid-priced state system. Table 2 shows the average undergraduate tuition for a year at Big Research U and a Regional College. Out-of-state tuition is a rough proxy for actual cost per student, so the difference between out-of-state and in-state is a rough proxy for the amount of state subsidy per student.[107] The substantially higher subsidy to Big Research U is used to fund its research function that the regional college does not have.

|  | In-State | Out-of-State | State Subsidy |
|---|---|---|---|
| Big Research U | 8,000 | 23,000 | 15,000 |
| Regional College | 6,000 | 15,000 | 9,000 |

So let's have the state say that any private college in the state whose admission standards are similar to Big Research U will get a $9,000 subsidy for in-state students so long as the private college's tuition, less subsidy, is equal to or lower than Big Research U's in-state tuition. Assuming the state still wants research, it can keep on sending the same $6,000 research subsidy to Big Research U (there is no good reason to tie research funding to undergraduate enrollment). So the total state subsidy remains at $15,000—$6,000 goes to Big Research U as a research subsidy and $9,000 to private college as a student instructional subsidy.

Let's assume there is a private charter college that a citizen-student would really like to attend. With its current cost structure and private donation base, it could charge a tuition of $17,000. So the citizen-student chooses to go the private college. The state and the citizen-student both spend the same amount as at Big Research U, but the citizen-student is happier because his $8,000 now gets him the private college of his choice rather than Big Research U.

Many existing private colleges today actually run with average net tuitions well under $17,000. (This isn't obvious since most quote a high sticker price and then privately negotiate discounts on a student-by-student basis). So let's assume there is a private charter college that the citizens-student would really like to attend, and it can charge $13,000. The citizen-student is happier because with the state subsidy she can now go the private college of her choice, and her tuition bill has dropped from $8,000 to $4,000 ($13,000 - $9,000 instructional subsidy).

Now let's assume a private charter college operates as a Better/Cheaper College and only needs to charge $8,000 tuition. Now the citizen-student's net tuition is zero ($8,000 - $9,000). Without any additional expense to the state, the citizen-student now has a tuition-free education.

Obviously, the financial loser under this system is Big Research U. By losing a student, they have lost both the student's tuition and the instructional portion of the subsidy. So it is down $17,000, but of course it no longer has any of the costs of educating the student. It still has its research mission and still gets $6,000 for research.

Now what happens if every Big Research U undergrad decides to go to a private charter college? Let's assume Big Research U had 20,000 in-state undergraduates and all of them decide to go to a Better/Cheaper College. Total tuition savings for citizen-students are $180 million per year. Big Research U doesn't get any money for undergraduate instruction, but it still gets $120 million from the state to do research. Combine this with Federal grants and private contracts, and Big Research U is definitely a player in the research world (and 20,000 citizen-students get a quality college education tuition free).

The goal of the private charter college plan isn't to run the public colleges and universities out of the undergraduate instruction business. Rather, it is to pressure them to behave responsibly. Eliminating the pricing advantage the subsidy gives to public colleges and universities will put a lot of competitive pressure on them to improve quality and drop tuition.

Of course there is no reason to limit this public funding/private delivery approach to Big Research U. When applied across an entire state public education system, total tuition savings even in a medium size state will run over $1 billion a year. Low priced (or totally free) higher education is not a fantasy. It was the norm 30 years ago. It can be the norm tomorrow.

## Donors Can Change the Industry

Donors don't have to wait on government to create a competitive market place. While good public policy would be highly beneficial, much can be done under the current bad public policy. This is a great time for a social entrepreneur to implement a Better/Cheaper College. With the huge increases in tuition over the last 30 years, a private Better/Cheaper College can now be price competitive with in-state tuition at state-owned universities. Donors can have a huge impact by providing the venture capital to make this possible.

The amount of philanthropic support for higher education from both individuals and foundations is staggering. In 2008, total private giving to higher education was $30.1 billion. Even with the major financial down-turn, 2009 giving registered $27.85 billion.[108] Yet given this impressive level of giving, colleges have continued to raise prices. While private donations are often used for good purposes, the purpose is always a cost add-on. Colleges never stop trying to maximize revenues.

The only thing a donor can do now to lower costs for a student is to create a scholarship. This helps the scholarship recipient but does nothing to solve the basic problem—costs go up as rapidly as funding allows. To maximize the return on their donation, donors should use their money to support Better/Cheaper Colleges.

If you can't find one, then create one. The cost of a start-up college is not out of reach for many big donors. For example, CELS for 3,200 students requires a $50 million physical plant.[109] If you start on a much smaller scale with leased premises, you probably need $10-15 million to achieve accreditation and fund operating losses until you reach break-even. Rather than a de novo start-up, you might get in at a much lower cost if you "bought" an existing college that is struggling. In the next few years, there will be several opportunities as struggling colleges close campuses and sell off their physical plants. Now is a great time for a serious donor to create a new college or even a whole system of colleges.

## Do It Now

I have not included any suggestions for the federal government as to policies to promote Better/Cheaper. In fact, this book has been written as if Washington did not exist. This has been deliberate. It is not because I feel Washington is totally irrelevant.[110] Rather, it is because radical improvement in higher education is not dependent on Washington. Radical improvement is dependent on entrepreneurs—whether they be at new or existing colleges—making it happen.

While there may be room for improvement in federal education policy,[111] achieving vastly lower cost and higher quality does not require a comprehensive national education plan with widespread political buy-in. There is nothing in current policy that prohibits a college operating as a Better/Cheaper College. A Better/Cheaper College can be launched today. There is no need to wait on the federal government for action.

Today, the opportunities for higher education entrepreneurs are huge. The existing market is large. Better/Cheaper College provides vastly superior value to the student. Established competitors are strongly tied to the old model and will be slow to respond. There is no reason to wait.

While the potential benefits to higher education entrepreneurs are huge, the long-run benefits to society are vastly greater. Today's pioneers will unleash a "gale of creative destruction"[112] upon the whole higher education industry. As the pioneers prove successful, others will imitate them, both because the pioneer has demonstrated the merits of the new model and because the pioneer's success puts competitive pressure on under-performers to improve. Over the long-run, annual cost savings can run into the hundreds of billions, and all students will truly have access to "a complete and generous education."

## Now is the Time to Start

## Part IV: Making Better/Cheaper a Reality

# Endnotes

1. For example see: J.D. Baer, A. Cook, and S. Baldi, *The National Survey of America's College Students*. American Institute for Research, 2001; *Our Failing Heritage: Americans Fail a Basic Test on Their History & Institutions*, Intercollegiate Studies Institute, 2008; and T. Jackson, *The Lowering of Higher Education in America: Why Financial Aid Should Be Based on Student Performance*, Praeger, 2010.
2. For example see H.R. Lewis, *Excellence Without a Soul: How a Great University Forgot Education*. New York: PublicAffairs, 2006.
3. My CELS projection was $7,376. Actual cost will vary based on the specifics of an individual college pursing a Better/Cheaper model. In designing CELS I didn't cut any corners, so you could get to a somewhat lower number without seriously impacting quality. On the other hand, the cost would be about $2,000 higher for a small college with 1,000 students (there are modest economies of scale) or $2,000 lower for a pure commuter college, etc. So, for the sake of simplicity of presentation, in the rest of this book I use $8,000 as the cost of a Better/Cheaper College.
4. The Delta Cost Project. "Trends in College Spending," *The Delta Project on Postsecondary Education Costs, Productivity, and Accountability*. Web. 09 Sept. 2010. www.deltacostproject.org/analyses/delta_reports.asp>.
5. Organizational culture is defined as "a system of shared values (what is important) and beliefs (how things work) that interact with the organization's people, organizational structures, and systems to produce behavioral norms (the way we do things around here)." B. Uttal and J. Fierman, "The Corporate Culture Vulture," *Fortune*, 17 Oct. 1983: 66-73.
6. D.C. Bok, *Our Underachieving Colleges: a Candid Look at How Much Students Learn and Why They Should Be Learning More*. Princeton, NJ: Princeton UP, 2006: 35.
7. J. Milton, *Of Education*. Eugene, OR: University of Oregon Scholars' Bank, 2005.
8. R.G. Douthat, "The Truth About Harvard," T*he Atlantic Monthly*. Mar. 2005. Web. 23 Aug. 2010. www.theatlantic.com/magazine/archive/2005/03/the-truth-about-harvard/3726/.
9. R.G. Douthat, *Privilege: Harvard and the Education of the Ruling Class*. New York: Hyperion, 2005.
10. M. Clifford, Conversation with author, 2009.
11. H.R. Lewis, *Excellence Without a Soul: How a Great University Forgot Education*. New York: Public Affairs. 2006: 25.
12. Bok, FN 6: 36-8.

13. L.R. Veysey, *The Emergence of the American University*. Chicago: University of Chicago Press, 1965.
14. J. Pierson, "The Left University," *The Weekly Standard,* 3 Oct. 2005.
15. A. Wolfe, "The Feudal Culture of the Postmodern University," *The Wilson Quarterly*, 20.1 (1996): 54.
16. H. Hansmann, *The Ownership of Enterprise*, Harvard University Press (1996); "The Changing Roles of Public, Private, and Nonprofit Enterprise in Education, Health Care, and Other Human Services," in V. Fuchs, *Individual and Social Responsibility: Child Care, Education, Medical Care and Long-Term Care in America*. University of Chicago Press, 1996: 245-275.
17. See for example N. Lemann, "What Harvard Taught Larry Summers: Elite Universities Serve the Faculty Better than the Students," *Time*, 26 Feb. 2006.
18. E.L. Carter and P. Fain. "Paychecks Top More than $1-Million for 23 Private-College Presidents," *The Chronicle*, 1 Nov. 2009.
19. F.N. Hansmann, 16. Also see the discussion of general education curriculum on pp. 11-14 of this book.
20. A. Manshel, "Why Top Colleges Squeeze You Dry." *Wall Street Journal*, 7 Apr. 2010.
21. H.R. Bowen, *The Costs of Higher Education*, National Book Network, 1980.
22. A similar view is called the academic ratchet and administrative lattice. See R. Zemsky, G.R. Wegner, and W.F. Massy, *Remaking the American University: Market-Smart and Mission-Centered*. Rutgers University Press, 2005; A. Ortmann and R. Squire, "A Game-Theoretic Explanation of the Administrative Lattice in Institutions of Higher Learning," *Journal of Economic Behavior & Organization*, 2000, 43.3: 377-391.
23. K. Carey, *College Rankings Reformed: The Case for a New Order in Higher Education*. Washington, DC: Education Sector, 2006: 1.
24. R.E. Martin, "The Revenue-to-Cost Spiral in Higher Education," *The John William Pope Center for Higher Education Policy*. Web. 9 Sept. 2010. www.popecenter.org/inquiry_papers/article.html?id=2196>.
25. This position was developed by Gordon Winston, an economics professor at Williams College.
26. Milton, FN7.
27. L. Ryken, *Worldly Saints: The Puritans as They Really Were*. Grand Rapids, MI: Zondervan, 1986: 169-170.
28. R. Khurana, *From Higher Aims to Hired Hands: The Social Transformation of American Business Schools and the Unfulfilled Promise of Management as a Profession*. Princeton University Press, 2007.

29. P. Berkowitz, "Our Compassless Colleges." *Wall Street Journal* 5 Sept. 2007.
30. Lewis, FN 11: 253.
31. *Northwest Ordinance* (1787), Sec. 14, Art. 3
32. R.K. Nieli, *From Christian Gentleman to Bewildered Seeker: The Transformation of Higher Education in America*. Raleigh, NC: John William Pope Center for Higher Education Policy, 2007: 3-4.
33. See F.N. Nieli, 32; G.M. Marsden, *The Soul of the American University*. Oxford University Press, 1994.
34. A.C. Guelzo, "Is There an American Mind?" NR/Digital, May 25, 2009.
35. D. D'Souza, *Illiberal Education: The Politics of Race and Sex on Campus*. New York: The Free Press, 1991.
36. V.H. Fried and A.D. Hill, "The Future of For-Profit Higher Education." *The Journal of Private Equity*, 12.4, 2009: 35-43.
37. R.L.Craig, J.R. Herman, and J.P. Anderson, *Post-Secondary Education Fact Book*, Stifel Nicolaus, 2008.
38. Fried & Hill, FN 36.
39. H. Hansmann, "Higher Education as an Associative Good," in M.n Devlin and J. Meyerson, eds., *Forum Futures: 1999 Papers*: 11-24.
40. I am using the tern IQ here to refer to general intellectual ability, not a specific measurement technique of general intellectual ability.
41. S. Goldberg, *Fads and Fallacies in the Social Sciences*. Amherst, NY: Humanity, 2003: 109-10. As summarized on pp. 109-110 of Murray, FN 45.
42. Murray argues that being in the top 10% is the intellectual equivalent of the 300 pound tackle (FN 45, p. 110). Others argue for the top 20% or 30%. These percentages are of the whole college age population, not just those taking college boards. For a discussion of the relationship between IQ, education and career performance, see L. Gottfredson, "Where and Why G Matters: Not a Mystery," *Human Performance*, 15.1, 2002: 25-46, particularly Figure 2 on p. 40.
43. "Jim Collins - Video/Audio - The Hedgehog Concept," *Jim Collins - Home*. Web. 25 Aug. 2010. www.jimcollins.com/media_topics/hedgehog-concept.html>.
44. R. Steele, "The Tradesmen's Calling," as quoted in Ryken, FN 27: 26.
45. C. Murray, *Real Education: Four Simple Truths for Bringing America's Schools Back into Reality*. New York: Crown Forum, 2008: 106.
46. T. Wolfe, Foreword to R.H. Hersh and J. Merrow. *Declining by Degrees: Higher Education at Risk*. New York: Palgrave Macmillan, 2005.

47. S.B. Dale and A.B. Krueger, "Estimating the Payoff to Attending a More Selective College: An Application of Selection on Observables and Unobservables." 1999. Working paper no. 7322. National Bureau of Economic Research. Also see T. Evans, "Penn State Tops Recruiter Rankings," *The Wall Street Journal*, 13 Sept. 2010.
48. W. Deresiewicz, "The Disadvantages of an Elite Education," *The American Scholar,* Summer 2008. www.theamericanscholar.org/the-disadvantages-of-an-eilite-education..
49. The Boston Consulting Group. *A New World Order of Consumption*, June 2010.
50. P.J. Deenen, "When Campuses Became Dysfunctional," *Minding the Campus*. Web. 24 Aug. 2010. www.mindingthecampus.com/originals/2009/05/by_patrick_j_deneen_in.html>.
51. Often the order is reversed in practice. This is fine as long as there is a fit between the value proposition and the target market.
52. Bok, FN 6, p.42.
53. T. Sowell, *Inside American Education: the Decline, the Deception, the Dogmas*. New York: Free, 1993: 94.
54. P.S. Babcock and M. Marks, "The Falling Time Cost of College; Evidence from Half a Century of Time Use Data," 2010, Working paper no. 15954, National Bureau of Economic Research.
55. S.M. Young and D. Pinsky, 2006, "Narcissism and Celebrity," *Journal of Research in Personality*, 40: 463-471.
56. J.C. Bergman, J.W. Westerrnan, and J.P. Daly. "Narcissism in Management Education," *Academy of Management Learning & Education*, 2010, 9: 119-131.
57. "Curricular Power: Explaining the Value of the Liberal Arts to Prospective Students and Their Parents," *GDA-Integrated Services, Student Recruitment and Enrollment Services and Consulting for Higher Education*. 24 Aug 2010. www.dchne.com/>.
58. "Another Look at the Future of Private College," *GDA-Integrated Services, Student Recruitment and Enrollment Services and Consulting for Higher Education*. 24 Aug. 2010. www.dehne.com/
59. For example, see R. Zemsky, "How to Save 25 Percent on College Tuition," *Newsweek*, October 17 2009.
60. Lewis, FN 2: 25
61. "Leader's Training Course | GoArmy.com." *Go Army Homepage | GoArmy.com*. 24 Aug. 2010. www.goarmy.com/rotc/leaders_training.jsp>.
62. For an overview of different views on Christian higher education, see C.W. Hoeckley, Liberal Arts and Christian Higher Education, Institute for the Liberal Arts at Westmont.

63. Marsden, FN 33: 17.
64. R. Kirk, *The Roots of American Order.* LaSalle, IL: Open Court, 1974.
65. For an example of the curriculum design for economic education see W.J. McLean, *Two Essays on Increasing the Learning Effectiveness of Economics Education.* 2010 DISS. Oklahoma State University, Stillwater: ProQuest LLC, 2010.
66. C. Christenson, *Disrupting Class: How Disruptive Innovation Will Change the Way the World Learns,* 2008, McGraw-Hill: 31.
67. M. Clifford, Conversation with author. 2009.
68. See p. 68 of this book.
69. K. Hampson, "Higher Ed Marketing: An Interview with John Lawler," *Higher Education Management Press* 24, July 2010.
70. Lewis, FN 2.
71. R. Vedder, "Why We Cannot Afford the Status Quo," Center for College Affordability and Productivity Blog, January 10, 2009. collegeaffordability.blogspot.com/2009_01_01_archive.html.
72. C. Miller, "Take a Hard Look, and Weed Out Weak Programs." *The Chronicle of Higher Education.* 9 July 2009. 24 Aug. 2010.
73. D. Jones and J. Wellman, "Bucking Conventional Wisdom on College Costs." *Inside Higher Ed.* 20 July 2009. Web. www.insidehighered.com/views/2009/07/20/wellmanjones>.
74. L.D. Fink, *Creating Significant Learning Experiences: An Integrated Approach to Designing College Courses.* San Francisco, CA: Jossey-Bass, 2003: xi.
75. C.A. Trigg, "Improving Quality and Reducing Costs: The Case for Redesign" in *Course Corrections: Experts Offer Solutions to the College Credit Crisis,* R.C. Dickeson, ed., Lumina Foundation for Education, 2005. For more recent illustration at a different college, see P.M. Turner, "Next Generation Course Redesign." *Change* 2009: 10-16.
76. *Business Strategy Game Simulation.* McGraw-Hill/Irwin, Inc. Web. 24 Aug. 2010. www.bsg-online.com/help/instructors/overview.html>.
77. "How U.S. News Calculates the College Rankings, *US News and World Report.* 24 Aug. 2010. www.usnews.com/articles/education/best-colleges/2010/08/17/ how-us-news-calculates-the-college-ranking.html?PageNr=4>.
78. The amount of faculty time physically in the class room and in preparation for class does not increase with enrollment.
79. *Team Based-Learning.* 24 Aug. 2010. teambasedlearning.apsc.ubc.ca/>.

80. For example, see U.S. Department of Education, Office of Planning, Evaluation, and Policy Development, *Evaluation of Evidence-Based Practices in Online Learning: A Meta-Analysis and Review of Online Learning Studies,* Washington, D.C., 2009.

81. D.L. Bennett, A.R Lucchesi, and R.K. Vedder. *For-Profit Higher Education: Growth, Innovation and Regulation.* Rep. Washington, D.C.: Center for College Affordability and Productivity, 2010. July 2010. 24 Aug. 2010. www.centerforcollegeaffordability.org/uploads/For Profit_HigherEd.pdf

82. "Strong Faculty Engagement in Online Learning". APLU Reports | The Sloan Consortium." 24 Aug. 2010. sloanconsortium.org/publications/survey/APLU_Reports

83. A finite sequence of instructions, an explicit, step-by-step procedure for solving a problem, often used for calculation and data processing. It is formally a type of effective method in which a list of well-defined instructions for completing a task, will when given an initial state, proceed through a well-defined series of successive states, eventually terminating in an end-state algorithms.

84. All the numbers in this paragraph are based on my own crude analysis. I am unaware of any published empirical study that directly addresses this topic.

85. Most of the concepts in this chapter concerning university endowments are based on H. Hansmann, "Why Do Universities Have Endowments?" *The Journal of Legal Studies,* 1990, 19.1: 3-42. The polemic tone is my own.

86. Hansmann, FN 85.

87. See A. Ortman, "The Nature and Causes of Corporate Negligence, Sham Lectures, and Ecclesiastical Indolence: Adam Smith on Joint-Stock Companies, Teachers, and Preachers." *History of Political Economy,* 1999, 31.2: 297-315.

88. In addition to the material included here, this book provides an excellent general framework for strategy analysis and a comprehensive discussion of entrepreneurial new games. A. Afuah, *Strategic Innovation: New Game Strategies for Competitive Advantage.* London: Routledge, 2009.

89. M.M. Crow, "Building an Entrepreneurial University." Speech. Third Annual Kauffman Foundation-Max Planck Institute Entrepreneurship Research Conference. Munich, Germany. 8 June 2008. Arizona State University. Web. president.asu.edu/sites/default/files/Building%20an%20Entrepreneurial%20University%20(Germany)%20060808%20Kauffman-Planck%20Conference_0.pdf>.

90. J.C. Strauss and J.R. Curry. *Responsibility Center Management: Lessons from 25 Years of Decentralized Management.* Washington, D.C.:

National Association of College and University Business Officers, 2002.
91. Crow, FN 89.
92. L.L. Bryan and C. Jones, "The 21st-century Organization," *The McKinsey Quarterly* 3 (2005): 25-33.
93. G. Leef, "Clarion Call: Term Limits for Tenure," *The John William Pope Center for Higher Education Policy*. 3 Mar. 2009. www.popecenter.org/clarion_call/article.html?id=2146>.
94. Leef, FN 91.
95. M.D. Cohen and J.G. March, *Leadership and Ambiguity. the American College President.* New York: McGraw Hill Book, 1974.
96. J.C. Collins and W.C. Lazier, *Beyond Entrepreneurship: Turning Your Business into an Enduring Great Company.* Prentice Hall, 1992.
97. Sowell, FN 53: 294-5
98. D.H. Maister, *The Anatomy of a Consulting Firm.* 2004. Web. davidmaister.com/articles/4/2/>.
99. Lewis, FN 11: 101
100. "Profession," *Wikipedia, the Free Encyclopedia.* Web. en.wikipedia.org/wiki/Profession>. For a more detailed definition, see A. Von Nordenflycht, "What Is a Professional Service Firm? Toward a Theory and Taxonomy of Knowledge-Intensive Firms," *Academy of Management Review* 35 (2009): 155-74.
101. A.W. Chickering, J.C. Dalton, and L. Stamm Auerbach. *Encouraging Authenticity and Spirituality in Higher Education.* San Francisco, CA: Jossey-Bass, 2006.
102. Karen Armstrong as quoted in: Chickering, FN 101.
103. Computed for an upper division business student taking 16 hours per semester.
104. For a theoretical overview of the entrepreneurial process combing both economic and behavioral perspectives see J. McMullen and D.A. Shepherd, "Entrepreneurial Action and the Role of Uncertainty in the Theory of the Entrepreneur," *Academy of Management Review* 31.1 (2006): 132-52. For a general discussion of the why central planning doesn't work, see F.A. Hayek, "The Use of Knowledge in Society," *The American Economic Review* 35 (1945): 519-30.
105. See K. Carey, "Living in a Post-NCLB World, Part II." *The Quick and the Ed.* Education Sector, 7 July 2010. Web. www.quickanded.com/2010/07/living-in-a-post-nclb-world-part-ii.html>. For a discussion of this point as it applies to K-12 education see F.M. Hess, *Education Unbound: The Promise and Practice of Greenfield Schooling,* ASCD

(2010). For a broad theological discussion of the role of regulation (the Law), see the writings of Paul, particularly Romans 3:19-20.

106. For a discussion of innovation in large organizations, see P. Skarzynski and R. Gibson, *Innovation to the Core: a Blueprint for Transforming the Way Your Company Innovates*. Boston, MA: Harvard Business School, 2008. Also see F.N. Hess, 105 for a discussion of how to foster innovation in K-12 education.

107. Actual cost data that is available does not break down costs between graduate and undergraduate education. In addition, the amount of subsidy may be slightly overstated depending on universities specific techniques for allocating donated income and other non-subsidy items as well as tuition discounts. However, it does not include interest charges born by the state to finance college buildings. Overall the differential makes for a reasonable, readily available, proxy for the subsidy. Indeed, some state college systems explicitly price by setting out-of-state tuition at actual cost and then deducting state subsidy to arrive at in-state tuition.

108. Council for Aid to Education. *Contributions to Colleges and Universities Down 11.9 Percent to $27.85 Billion: Greatest Decline Ever Recorded*. 3 Feb. 2010.

109. See pp. 165 of this book, and assuming local government sharing $20 million of the costs of multipurpose arena and stadium.

110. In fact, federal higher education policies may have been a major factor in the rapid run-up in tuition, e.g., see R.K. Vedder, *Going Broke by Degree: Why College Costs Too Much*. Washington, D.C.: AEI, 2004.

111. Two major questions are: "Has federal spending on higher education lead to higher prices? and "Are the accrediting agencies acting as a cartels to protect ITC profits?" More fundamentally, "Does the federal government have any proper role in education at any level?"

112. J.A. Schumpeter, *Capitalism, Socialism, and Democracy*, New York: Harper & Brothers, 1942.

# Index

## A

Academic Ethic—see Ivory Tower
active learning 66
advising 58-59
Afuah, Allan 81
alumni 34, 71
Amacher, Ryan 86
American Order 48-49
Amherst 68

amoral colleges 25, 28
Anderson, Charles 15
Arizona State University 83
Army *ROTC 46*
Arts & Sciences majors 54-55
associate's degree 45-46
authority of professor 15

## B

bachelor's degree 36, 45-46
barriers to response 2, 6
Berkowitz, Peter 27
biology major 54-55
Bob Jones University 49, 102
Bok, Derek 9, 14, 41, 47
Bowen, Howard 19, 21, 22

Bowen's Laws
    original statement *19-21*
    Martin's elaboration 21-23
brain surgeon 90-91
bricks and mortar 71-72
Brockman, Kent 54
Brown University 52
*Business Strategy Game (The)* 67

## C

Carey, Kevin 21
CELS (College of Entrepreneurial
    Leadership and Society) 4-5, 41-
    42, 45, 55
Christenson, Clayton 52
Christianity and higher education
    28-31, 48-49, 101-103
church college 48-49
class size 67-69, 57-58, 70
Clifford, Michael 12, 56-57
Collins, Jim 35, 88
commuter college 34, 42

*Creating Significant Learning
    Experiences* 65-66
credentialing 33, 42
Crow, Michael M. 83
culture
    encouraging professional
    behavior 92-93
    also see "Ivory Tower"
curriculum design
    knowledge/skills/abilities 51,
    54-55
    mass customization and
    modular design 52-53

## D

decision making processes 18-19, 88-90
*Declining by Degrees* 37
Deneen, Patrick, 39
Deresiewicz, William, 38
Dienstig, Jules 55
*Different Strokes for Different Folks* 36

*Disrupting Class: How Disruptive Education Will Change the Way the World Works* 52
donors as change agents 111-112, also see endowments
Douthat, Ross 12
D'Souza, Dinsesh 31-32
Duke 12
DuPont University 49

## E

*Ecclesiastes* 79
endowments 72-79
entrepreneurial behavior 1-2, 6, 99, 101, 106-107, 112-113

*Excellence Without a Soul* 28
excess compensation 5, 18, 92

## F

faculty
    values 91-92
    compensation 92
    reducing headcount 98
*Faulty Towers: Tenure and the Structure of Higher Education* 86
featherbedding 5, 18, 67-68, 98
federal government 112
feudal system 15-16

Fink, L. Dee 65
Flintstone, Fred 74
for-profit colleges 5, 69, 103
for-profit managers/non-profit owners 104
*From Christian Gentlemen to Bewildered Seeker: The Transformation of Higher Education in America* 29-30

## G

garbage can model 88
general education curriculum 11-14, 43
general technical education 43-44
German research university 15, 30

George A. Dehne Associates 44
Georgetown 40
Goldberg, Steven 35
Grand Canyon University 12, 56-57

## H

Hansmann, Henry 72, 74-75
Harvard University
    general education curriculum 12-14
    founding purpose 9, 28
    as goal of prestige segment 37

    as amoral institution 38
high school, 46
Higher Learning Commission, 11-12
history of colleges 15-16, 28-31

## I

IQ 35
illiberal colleges 31-32
*Illiberal Education* 31
instructional methods 65-69
intellectual elitism 34-35
Ivory Tower
    Learning for Learning's sake 9
    impact on curriculum 11-14
    Impact on organization 14-16

Ivory Tower Collective
    defined 19
    collective decision making 18-19
    ownership of colleges 5, 17-19, 87-90
    also see "ITC profits"
ITC profits
    eliminating as key to Better/ Cheaper 5-6, 17, 23
    also see "profits"

## J

Jefferson, Thomas 10

John William Pope Center for Higher Education Policy 86

## K

Khurana, Rakesh 26

*Killing the Spirit* 87

## L

land-grant university 62
learning
    as means to better life 9-11, 25-26
    for its own sake 9
Leef, George 86-87
Lewis, Harry 13, 28, 58, 91

liberal education
    defined 25-26
    and moral values 26, 32
    amoral colleges 28-31
    decline 30-31
    in 21st Century 47-49
    at state universities 101-103
    loose graduates 26-28

## M

Madison James, 10
Mafia Honor Code 16
Maister, David 90
Maister's Matrix of Professional Work 90-91
March, James 88
market segments 33-37
market share 16, 103

Martin Robert E. *21*
MBA 26
Meiners, Roger 86
Milton, John 9, 25-26
Michigan State University 43
multi-college universities 101-103
Murray, Charles 36

# Index

## N

narcissism 42
Natural Law 47-48
Nieli, Russell K. 29
Nisbet, Robert E. 29

non-profits
  legal form 17
  ITC ownership 19-19
  also see "profits"
Northwest Ordinance 28
nurse 90-91

## O

*Of Education* 9-10
Oklahoma State University 61-62
online education 69-71

opportunities in higher education
  1-2, 87-88, 101, 103-104, 111-112
*Our Underachieving Colleges* 2

## P

Pennsylvania State University 2
people 90-93
personalizing education 55-59
Piereson, James 14
Politically Correct University 26
president 18, 98-100
prestige-oriented segment 37-40
Princeton 37, 40
professional services firm 90-93
profits
  defined 5
  maximizing as goal of college 17, 25

 profitability of non-profits 5, 18
raising prices to increase profits 23
also see "ITC profits"
*Proverbs* 36, 77
psycholohy major 54-55
public service mission 62-63
Puritans 28, 30, 36, also see "Milton, John"
purpose of education 9-11, 25-26

## Q

quadrivium 29

## R

research
  conflict with achieving Better/Cheaper 59-63
  managing in a research university 84-85
  in a state system 109-110

Responsibility Centered Management 84
Rockfish Gap 10
Roxbury free school 28
Ryken, Leland 25

# Index

## S

Saint John Doe College 76-79
scholarships 74, 77-79, 111
Simon, Herb 88
Simpsons 54
Slippery Rock 60
small private colleges
   competing with state flagships 97-98
   managing in best interest of students 98, 100
   president 98, 100
   trustees 98, 100
   program elimination process 99-100
Smith, Adam 78
Smith, Page 87
socialization as part of value proposition 46
Solomon 36
Sowell, Thomas 41, 88
Spirituality in Education 102
state governments
   cost of public education 104-106
   as cause of problem 106-107
   defunding higher education 107
   breaking up cartel 107-108
   private charter colleges 109-111
standardization of courses 53
*Strategic Innovation: New Game Strategies for Competitive Business Advantage* 81-82, 85-86, 90, 92
structure 82-85
students
   associative good 34
   role in production process 33, 57-58
   personal interactions with 56-57
   personal relations between 57-58
student/faculty ratio 67-68
systems/processes 85-90

## T

target market 33, 37, 49
Team Based Learning 58
tenure 86-88
time to graduate 45-46
trivium 29
Trophy Generation, 39
trustees 98, 100
tuition increases 2-3, 104-105
Tulane 86

## U

undersubscribed course 63
University of Berlin 14
University of California-Santa Cruz 12
University of Massachusetts 38
University of Michigan 59
University of Phoenix 5
University of Virginia 10
U.S. News and World Report Ratings 21, 37, 68

## V

value proposition must-haves 41-43
value segment 34, 39-40
Vedder, Rich 59

Virginia Tech University 67
vocational education 45, 54-55

## W

Washington, DC 112
*Wealth of Nations* 78
Williams College 68

Wolfe, Alan 15
Wolfe, Tom 37, 49

## Y

Yale 28, 37

# Appendices

Appendix I presents the value proposition, curriculum, and operational overview for The College of Entrepreneurial Leadership and Society (CELS). CELS is the hypothetical college I created in order to determine the true cost of a high-quality residential education. It was originally published in "The $7,376 "Ivies": Value-Designed Models of Undergraduate Education."

Appendix II is a detailed statement of pro forma operating expenses for CELS. It was also originally published in "The 7,376 "Ivies." The difference between the $7,736 of the title and the $6,705 per student operating expenses reflected in the pro forma statement is due to an assumed 10% operating profit margin.

# Appendix I

# College of Entrepreneurial Leadership and Society (CELS)

## Value Proposition

**We will provide a useful education for a productive, balanced life.** We will target students who are willing and able to accept leadership roles. They will be interested in a broad education, avoiding both the vocational school and the "ivory tower." They will be interested in professional success, but feel there is more to life. While many students may be somewhat individualistic, they will feel a strong responsibility to society.

**We will provide a challenging and supportive environment.** We will want students to succeed, but believe that true success requires overcoming challenges. We will support our students but not baby them.

**We will provide meaningful learning experiences outside of the traditional classroom.** We will target traditional students who want to be actively involved in college life. We will ensure that they have meaningful out-of-class experiences as part of their education.

**We will focus on undergraduate education.** While graduate education, research, and public service may be good missions, they will not be our mission. We will not use undergraduate education to subsidize other missions. We will not allow any of these missions to detract in any way from undergraduate education.

**We will provide the best value for our target market.** We will not try to attract the status-driven student or parent, nor will we try to be the lowest-priced route to a college degree. We will understand that wasteful spending raises costs, not quality. Our goal will be to provide a reasonably priced education of equivalent or better quality than high-priced colleges.

## Curriculum

CELS will have a broad curriculum that will provide students with appropriate technical skills for entry-level jobs, potential to be a general manager of an organization early in their careers, understanding of the "big picture," and foundational skills and knowledge for life outside of work. With sufficient student demand, programs will be offered in business, behavioral science, communication arts, education, engineering science, information technology, letters and civilization (interdisciplinary humanities), public affairs, and science and technology. These programs will not only teach technical skills and current trends, but will also give students an understanding of the institutional, social, and intellectual histories of the profession as well as its ethical and social responsibilities. (Appendix A is a list of CELS degree requirements and courses.)

Approximately 50% of the curriculum will be required courses for all students. This will include several interdisciplinary humanities/social sciences courses as well as a smaller set of entrepreneurial leadership courses. Another 30% will be a core curriculum based on the professional program. To allow students to customize their education, the remaining 20% of the curriculum will consist of electives from the student's professional concentration, a minor area, or any other concentrations that match the student's career goals and personal interests. Unlike most colleges, CELS will require its students to complete a significant, individually designed mix of out-of-class experiences (e.g., cocurricular activities, travel, jobs) supported by formalized faculty mentoring.

## Educational Processes

CELS's educational processes will be built upon existing best practices. CELS will be a leader in integrating and implementing these practices. Major best practices include the following.

- Involving students in the campus community. Students involved in the college community are more committed to the educational process and tend to learn more.
- Using common course design. The widely used one-off approach involves a great deal of duplication of faculty work and produces wide variance from section to section in student learning.[1]
- Focusing on credit hours, not contact hours. A four-credit-hour class does not necessarily require four contact hours a week with faculty. The issue is the hours of effort required by a student, not the number of hours the student is in a classroom with a faculty member.
- Using technology wisely. Proper use of advanced instructional technology saves a lot of money. Technology is particularly helpful for course management, as well as for the "content dump" (e.g., podcast lectures) and "drill and kill" (e.g., programmed learning) components of instruction. But even in courses like introductory math that are almost pure "drill and kill," many students benefit from having moderate structure and readily available personal assistance.[2]

# Appendix I

- Using high-participation/application teaching techniques for learning both basic content and higher-level application skills. The case method has long been used successfully in law and business schools. More recently, team-based learning has been used in a variety of disciplines.[3] While it may sound similar, team-based learning is very different from "student-centric" techniques involving loosely focused class group work. With team-based learning, tightly focused small group and all-class discussions are blended in a single class period. By working in 5–7 person teams, students are forced to be actively involved in learning both content and application. A team-based learning class of 100 generates more in-class involvement than a traditional lecture class of 19, at a drastically lower cost.

- Using small classes sparingly. Small classes are necessary if the student's work in a course needs to be highly customized. In most courses, however, small class size is not necessary, nor does increase student benefits. Small classes are a disaster from a cost standpoint, so they should be held only when there is a strong and clear student benefit.

- Using small cohorts to create community. Use of big classes with small cohorts builds community better than small classes with large cohorts, and at a significantly lower cost. This is the approach long taken by major law schools and graduate business schools that divide incoming first-year students into groups of about 100. Students then take all their first-year courses only with students in their section. While class size is relatively large, community is created because the same 100 people are in each class.

- Providing top-notch advising. For a minimal additional cost, excellent career, academic, and personal advising service significantly increase the ability to customize students' education and increase their satisfaction and commitment.

- Using off-campus programs to provide specialized training and enrich the educational experience. If foundational courses are strong, a limited amount of off-campus programming adds a great deal of educational flexibility.

CELS will use all of these best practices. All courses other than tutorials, field projects, and independent studies will be commonly designed. Technology will be used aggressively where appropriate. The campus will be wireless and all students will be provided with a laptop. Class management will be totally computerized, and podcast lectures and programmed learning will be used where appropriate.

Given the nature of CEL's value proposition, most of the curriculum will be built around high-participation/application courses. Small classes under 10 will only be used early in the required communications course and some basic personal skills development classes, and later in formalized mentoring and field projects.

The CELS approach to teaching will not only be highly cost-effective, but also highly personal due to its targeted use of small classes and heavy use of team-based learning. Key to the management of the student's junior and senior years will be the area of concentration tutorial. Every semester, junior and senior students will take a one-hour tutorial with up to five other students with similar career interests. Through the tutorial, the student's mix of courses, out-of-class learning experiences, and job or graduate school searches will be formalized and mentored by a faculty member who is qualified to provide personalized academic and career advice.

In addition to a required internship, students will also be able to look outside the walls of CELS for specialty course work that CELS will not offer. Because the required course work ensures that students will receive a strong and broad foundation, CELS will be able to allow its students flexibility in pursuing off-campus learning opportunities. Of particular interest will be the numerous relatively open-enrollment ("special student" status), short-term courses, especially those offered in the summer.

Many major universities offer a good selection of upper-division courses coupled with special student enrollment options in the summer. Further, offering short-term intensive courses is not limited to traditional American educational institutions. For example, CELS students desiring to improve their language skills and cultural knowledge will be able to attend a summer language institute in a country where that language is dominant. Similarly, students wanting advanced study in film-making will be able to take the basic courses at CELS and then spend a summer in Los Angeles at a film academy, or public affairs students will be able to take a specialty course and internship in DC through the nonprofit Washington Center or several other fellowship programs. While prices for these outside courses are above CELS rates, they are competitive with most private schools' regular session rates and even cheaper than some. Paying higher tuition for 6–12 hours of a college degree is a lot cheaper than paying high rates for all 128. These specialty off-campus programs can add value by giving students experiences they cannot receive through traditional on-campus education. In addition, by taking advantage of off-campus programs in the summer, an academically ambitious student will be able to graduate in three years.

## Student Life

A major component of the educational process at CELS will be a house system, somewhat along the lines of the residential colleges at Harvard and Yale.[4] Every freshman will be randomly assigned to a house they will belong to for all four years. Houses will be same-sex and have 150–225 members, including about 50 entering freshmen a year. The house will be the primary social unit for the student while in college. In this regard, the house will function somewhat like a Greek house, with a high level of student management, but within a clear framework established by CELS. Students will be required to live in the house for their first two or three years. Students living outside of the house will still participate in house activities, including weekly house dinners.

In addition to internal social functions, the house will be the primary unit for student participation in a variety of broad-interest student life activities like intramural sports, general community service projects, "varsity revue," and homecoming. (Special interest student activities will generally be done at the college rather than the house level. e.g., professsional clubs, religious organizations, student newspapers, Young Democrats/Republicans, jazz band, etc.) High student involvement in the activities of these self- governing houses will be central to the CELS value proposition.

The house will also be the delivery point for the required personal skills development courses taken during the freshman and sophomore years. As part of their personal development course, students will be required to participate in a variety of ways in the activities and management of the house.

Each house will have a faculty member who serves as senior tutor. The senior tutor will actively advise the house government and ensure that the house is operating within the framework established by CELS. In addition to advising the house government, the senior tutor will play a major role in every house member's academic and personal development, particularly during the first two years. The senior tutors will be the academic and personal advisors for all freshmen and sophomores in their houses, and will also be responsible for the personal skills development courses for their houses. Upperclassmen will serve as junior tutors, assisting the senior tutor with certain house responsibilities.

A group of 6–7 freshmen will live in the same part of the house with their assigned junior tutor. Junior tutors will assist the senior tutor in providing a structured program of personal development and academic counseling for their tutorial groups. The junior tutors' formal structured roles will include serving as group facilitators in the personal development course, personal mentors on some personal development skills (e.g., time management), and mentor/monitor of participation in student life activities in both the house and college. In addition, each underclass student will have an informal personal mentor who is a junior or senior member of the house.

In addition to the senior tutor's formal roles in the house, he or she will provide a great deal of informal encouragement and guidance. The senior tutor will have an office in and eat a majority of meals at the house. In addition, every regular faculty member will serve as a fellow of a house, promoting communication between faculty and students. This results in 4–

5 faculty fellows for per house. The fellows' role will be informal but will require regular attendance at house dinners and major house activities.

## Staffing

CELS will have fewer faculty members than a traditional institution, but its faculty will be top-notch. CELS faculty will be generalists with a strong commitment to the CELS model. CELS will have three types of full-time faculty: professors, teaching fellows, and senior tutors. Professors' and teaching fellows' primary duties will be teaching academic courses, includeing upper-division tutorials. Both groups will also be involved, in a relatively informal manner, with student life. Faculty will attend weekly house dinners, advise student clubs, and attend student events.

In addition, professors will be responsible for representing CELS to the academic, professional, and local communities. They will be subject-area thought leaders for CELS and may also have significant administrative responsibilities. A professor will serve as area coordinator for each academic area the college offers and will also play a significant role in overall institutional management. There will be at least one professor in each area. After that, the ratio of professors to teaching fellows in an area will be approximately 1-to-2.

At least one professor in each area will have a terminal degree. Other professors and teaching fellows may or may not have traditional academic credentials. In some areas, such as behavioral science, a Ph.D. will be the norm, but in others, such as business, many may possess a masters degree. No matter what level degree they have completed, all professors and teaching fellows will possess and maintain high subject matter expertise, practical experience, and the ability to communicate with undergraduates.

As part of representing CELS to the academic community, professors will be given a limited amount of release time to do research. All faculty with traditional academic backgrounds will be able to pursue part-time traditional research activities independent of CELS. All faculty will be required to do a modest amount of public service. In addition to research and public service, CELS will strongly encourage faculty to engage in other types of professional activities (e.g., consulting) independent of CELS. CELS will allow faculty to be on three-quarter or half-time status as long as they fully discharge their CELS duties.

Senior tutors are vital to the success of the house system. Like regular faculty, senior tutors will be both reflective and action-oriented. They will not be traditional faculty' however, as they will be chosen for their ability to promote the general welfare and personal development of undergraduates. Most senior tutors will have a masters degree with at least four years of work experience. About 60% of a senior tutor's time will be devoted to house responsibilities and managing the personal skills development courses. The remainder of his or her time will be devoted to teaching and/or more traditional staff roles.

Adjunct faculty will be used primarily to cover niches. Unlike most schools, CELS will not use adjuncts as a cost reduction tactic. The CELS adjunct will be someone in the community with specialized knowledge and expertise who enjoys teaching one or two courses a year.

## Exhibit A
## CELS Degree Requirements and Courses[5]

All courses are for four credit hours unless otherwise indicated.[6] Some courses are shown more than once if required in more than one area or if they would be an appropriate elective in another area.

| Core | |
|---|---|
| Civilization: Historical Perspective | |
| Civilization: Institutions & Individuals I | |
| Civilization: Institutions & Individuals II | |
| Civilization: Literature & Fine Arts | |
| Civilization: Theology & Philosophy | |
| Civilization: International Comparisons | |
| Lifespan of Human Development | |
| Thinking Skills | 6 |
| Personal Skills Development | 4(1)* |
| Communication Skills | |
| Science of Everyday Things OR other science | |
| Entrepreneurial Management | 6 |
| Personal Finance | 2 |
| Personal Law | 2 |
| **Total Required Core** | 56 |

*Four courses, each one hour long.

## Behavioral Science

*Required:*

Two of the following:
| | |
|---|---|
| Child Development | 2 |
| Adolescent Development | 2 |
| Adult Development/Gerontology | 2 |

| | |
|---|---|
| Counseling Skills | 2 |
| Behavioral Research Methods I | 2 |
| Psychopathology I | 2 |
| Family Dynamics | 2 |
| Assessment & Observation | 2 |
| Social Work / Community Counseling | 2 |
| Social Policy | 2 |
| Managing Human Services | 2 |
| Behavioral electives (see right column) | 4 |
| Tutorial | 4(1)* |
| Internship | |
| **Total Required** | **40** |

*Electives:*
| | |
|---|---|
| History of Psychology | |
| Behavioral Research Methods II | 2 |
| Criminology | 2 |
| Psychopathology II | 2 |
| Substance Abuse | 2 |
| Non-Normative Development | 2 |
| Family Therapy | |
| Psychology & Religion | |

*Four courses, each one hour long.

## Business

*Required:*

| | |
|---|---|
| Intermediate Economics | |
| Operations Management & Information Systems | |
| Financial Accounting & Management | |
| Marketing | 2 |
| Law & Management | 2 |
| Business Research Methods | |
| Business Models & Opportunity Development | |
| Strategic Management Process | |
| Finance & Capital Markets | |
| Field Project | |
| Internship | |
| Tutorial | 4(1)* |
| **Total Required** | **44** |

*\*Four courses, each one hour long.*

*Electives:*

| | |
|---|---|
| Intermediate Accounting I | |
| Intermediate Accounting II | |
| Advanced Entrepreneurship & Business Development | 2 |
| International Business | |
| Real Estate | |
| Investments | |
| Portfolio Management | 2 |
| Banking | 2 |
| Retailing | 2 |
| Services Management | 2 |
| Sports Management | 2 |
| Nonprofit Management | 2 |
| Promotions | |
| Personal Selling | 2 |
| Sales Management | 2 |
| Human Resources | 2 |

## Communication Arts

*Required:*

| | |
|---|---|
| Communications Performance I | |
| Media and Society | |
| Visual Media I | 2 |
| Sight & Sound | |
| Creative Writing | 2 |
| Writing for Media | |
| Reporting & Editing | 2 |
| Communications Law & Ethics | 2 |
| Tutorial | 4(1)* |
| Field Project | |
| Internship | |
| Communications Electives (see right column) | 12 |
| **Total Required** | **40** |

*Electives:*

| | |
|---|---|
| Communications Performance II | |
| Creative Writing II | |
| Feature Writing | 2 |
| Digital Filmmaking | |
| Linguistics | |
| Visual Media II | |
| Marketing | 2 |
| Public Relations | 2 |
| Promotions | |
| Advertising | 2 |
| Music Skills | |
| Music Skills II | |
| Visual Arts Studio | 8(1)** |

*Four courses, each one hour long.
**One hour studio courses that can be repeated 8 times.

## Education

| | | |
|---|---|---|
| *Required, 6-12:* | *Required, K-5:* | |
| Foundations of Education | Foundations of Education | |
| Learning Theory & Course Design | Learning Theory & Course Design | 2 |
| Measurement & Evaluation | 2 | Measurement & Evaluation | 2 |
| Educating the Exceptional Child | 2 | Educating the Exceptional Child | 2 |
| Student Teaching | 12 | Student Teaching | 12 |
| Tutorial | 4(1)* | Tutorial | 4(1)* |
| Adolescent Development | 2 | Child Development | 2 |
| Teaching Methods for 6-12 | | Teaching Methods for Early Childhood | |
| Content area courses vary | | Teaching Methods for Elementary | |
| | | Child & Adolescent Literature | 2 |
| | | Visual Media I | 2 |
| **Total Required** | **28+?** | **Total Required** | **42** |

*Four courses, each one hour long.*

## Engineering Science

| | |
|---|---|
| *Required:* | *Electives:* |
| Calculus I | Civil & Environmental Engineering  2 |
| Calculus II | Electrical Engineering  2 |
| Calculus III & Differential Equations | Computer & Electrical Engineering  2 |
| Computer Programming I | Mechanical Engineering  2 |
| General Chemistry I | Chemical Engineering  2 |
| General Physics I | |
| General Physics II | |
| Introduction to Engineering Design  2 | |
| Introduction to Engineering Systems  2 | |
| Advanced Engineering Design | |
| Advanced Engineering Systems | |
| Chemical & Thermal Processes | |
| Continuum Mechanics | |
| Circuits & Digital Electronics | |
| Engineering Electives (see right column)  1 | |
| Tutorial  4(1)* | |
| Field Project | |
| Internship | |
| **Total Required**  64 | |

*Four courses, each one hour long.

## Information Technology

*Required:* | | *Electives:* | |
---|---|---|---
Calculus I | | Advanced Decision-Making Technology | 2
Operations Management & Information Systems | | Advanced Data Exploitation | 2
Computer Programming I | | E-Commerce | 2
Computer Programming II | | Organizational Strategy & Information Systems | 2
Systems Analysis & Design | | Advanced Computer Science | |
Database Management & Exploitation | | | |
Data Communication | 2 | | |
Decision Making Technologies | 2 | | |
Tutorials | 4(1)* | | |
Field Project | | | |
Internship | | | |
**Total Required** | **40** | | |

*Four courses, each one hour long.

## Letters and Civilization

*Required:*

| | |
|---|---|
| Christianity | |
| Literary Classics | |
| Historical Inquiry | 2 |
| Literary Analysis | 2 |
| Letter & Civilization electives (see right column) | 14 |
| History (at least) | 4 |
| English (at least) | 4 |
| Theology/Philosophy (at least) | 2 |
| Senior Paper | |
| Minor (includes Tutorial and Internship) | 20 |
| **Total Required** | **54** |

*Electives:*

History (all 2 hours)
African-American
Gilded Age to Great Depression
American Frontier
State & Local History
World War II
Post–World War II America
American Civil War
Women in History
Classical                                                                    4

*Electives (continued):*

Medieval
Renaissance & Reformation
Modern European
English (all 2 hours unless indicated)
Shakespeare & Contemporaries
19th Century Literature
20th Century Literature
Current Authors
Lyrics
Creative Nonfiction
Theater I
Theater II
Film I
Film II
Television
Theology/Philosophy (all 2 hours)
New Testament
Old Testament
History of Philosophy
World Religions
The Two Cities

*Four courses, each one hour long.

## Public Affairs

| | | |
|---|---|---|
| *Required:* | | *Electives:* |
| Intermediate Economics | | Advanced Policy Research Methods |
| Policy Analysis & Formulation | | Political Campaigns |
| Political Economy | 2 | Community Development |
| Comparative Systems | | |
| American Government | | |
| Public Administration | 2 | |
| International Relations | 2 | |
| Current Domestic Policy Issues | | |
| Current Foreign Policy Issues | | |
| Tutorial | 4(1)* | |
| Field Study | | |
| Internship | | |
| **Total Required** | **42** | |

*Four courses, each one hour long.

## Science and Technology

*Required:*

| | |
|---|---|
| Calculus I | |
| Computer Programming I | |
| General Biology | |
| General Physics I | |
| General Chemistry I | |
| Environmental Science I | |
| Science & Technology or Engineering Sciences (see right column) | 8 |
| Tutorial | 4(1)* |
| Internship | |
| **Total Required** | **40** |

*Electives:*

| | |
|---|---|
| General Physics II | |
| General Chemistry II | |
| Organic Chemistry I | |
| Organic Chemistry II | |
| Human Physiology | |
| Cellular Biology | 2 |
| Genetics | 2 |
| Environmental Science II | |
| Environmental Science III | |

*Four courses, each one hour long.

# Appendix II

# Estimated Operating Expenses for CELS

**College of Entrepreneurial Leadership and Society Pro Forma Statement of Education & General (E&G) Operating Expenses**

| Activity | Total ($000) | Per FTE ($000) |
|---|---|---|
| Instruction | 7,571 | 2.366 |
| Research | 0 | 0.000 |
| Public Service | 0 | 0.000 |
| Academic Support | 3,703 | 1.157 |
| Student Services | 7,057 | 2.205 |
| Institutional Support | 3,126 | 0.977 |
| Total | 21,457 | 6.705 |

This pro forma statement was created using the build-up method. It assumes that CELS is a fully operational school with a stable enrollment of 3,200 students distributed across areas of concentration as follows.

**Concentration of Students**

| Concentration | # of Students |
|---|---|
| Education | 240 |
| Public Affairs | 400 |
| Letters & Civilization | 450 |
| Science & Technology | 170 |
| Engineering Science | 170 |
| Business | 800 |
| Communication Arts | 400 |
| Information Technology | 170 |
| Behavioral Science | 400 |
| Total | 3,200 |

It will be located in an area of the United States with an average cost of living. All buildings will be newly built at current building costs.

This pro forma statement follows standard accounting practice for colleges. It includes all operating expenses in what is often referred to as the educational and general primary budget. This is the number usually referred to when discussing educational cost per student. It does NOT include:

- revenues of any kind;
- institutionally funded scholarships (these are actually a price discount off tuition price);
- any financing expense;[7]
- expenses associated with sponsored research (e.g., research paid for by third parties like the NSF, NIH, or private industries);
- expenses of auxiliary activities such as dorms and bookstores, which are generally self-supporting and not viewed as educational costs.

Expenses are classified using standard activity categories for colleges.[8] To facilitate comparison with both public and private colleges, physical campus costs are treated as a separate category and then charged out to the other main cost categories.[9] Detailed statements with explanatory notes for each major activity follow.

## Instruction

| Expense | Total ($000) |
|---|---|
| Regular Faculty | 5,479 |
| Lab Faculty | 788 |
| Other Instructional | 211 |
| IT (Information Technology) | 212 |
| Depreciation | 344 |
| PPOM (Physical Plant Operations & Maintenance) | 536 |
| Total | 7,570 |

Faculty needs will be determined first by seeing how many course sections need to be offered in a year. Given the CELS commitment to offering 3-year accelerated degrees, at least one section of every course in the curriculum will be offered at least once a year. Multiple sections may be necessary based on enrollment. For example, with 800 first-year students and an enrollment cap of 100 per section, CELS will need to offer 8 sections a year of "Civilization: Historical Overview."

The first column in the table (Area) on the following page is the academic area of the course. The second column (Large) shows the number of regular course sections needed in a year. For example, I anticipate needing 25 sections of business in the year. In determining the number of sections, I assumed an enrollment cap of 100 per section (except for some communications classes, which will be capped at 25 or 50).

| | Regular Faculty | | | | | | | | | |
|---|---|---|---|---|---|---|---|---|---|---|
| | Sections | | | | | | Compensation | | | |
| Area | Large | Small | Total | Professors | Fellows | Adjuncts | Professor Comp. | Fellow Comp. | Adjunct Comp. | Total ($000) |
| Core | 104 | 0 | 104 | 6 | 13 | 0.3 | 105 | 67 | 32 | 1,509 |
| Behavioral Science | 14 | 8 | 22 | 1 | 3 | 0.0 | 105 | 65 | 32 | 301 |
| Business | 25 | 27 | 52 | 3 | 6 | 0.5 | 135 | 90 | 32 | 960 |
| Communication Arts | 24 | 13 | 37 | 2 | 4 | 0.7 | 95 | 60 | 32 | 451 |
| Education | 7 | 18 | 25 | 1 | 2 | 1.1 | 100 | 60 | 32 | 256 |
| Engineering Science | 11 | 6 | 17 | 1 | 2 | 0.1 | 110 | 80 | 32 | 273 |
| Information Technology | 9 | 6 | 15 | 1 | 1 | 0.6 | 120 | 80 | 32 | 219 |
| Letters & Civilization | 18 | 15 | 33 | 2 | 4 | 0.1 | 85 | 60 | 32 | 414 |
| Public Affairs | 13 | 13 | 26 | 1 | 3 | 0.5 | 115 | 75 | 32 | 357 |
| Science & Technology | 12 | 4 | 16 | 1 | 2 | -0.1 | 90 | 60 | 32 | 208 |
| Buffer | 22 | 15 | 37 | 2 | 5 | -0.1 | 105 | 65 | 32 | 531 |
| **Total** | **259** | **125** | **384** | **21** | **45** | **4** | — | — | — | **5,479** |

The next column (Small) is the number of small section courses needed. These will be small classes by design. Internships will not meet as a class but will require faculty supervision. "Class" size is estimated at 30 for internships and 4 for student teaching. The tutorials and field projects will be taught in very small sections, generally capped at 5. Due to their nature, these courses will require less faculty time than a traditional course. For example, a faculty member teaching a 4-hour field project class will only need to meet with the students an hour a week and spend about one hour a week outside of class. This is about one-quarter the amount of time necessary to teach a traditional class. So this column is stated in terms of traditional class teaching load equivalents. The actual number of small sections offered will be a little less than 4 times the amount shown.

The next column (Total) shows the number of total sections that need to be covered in both regular and small section equivalents. These sections will be covered by professors, teaching fellows, and adjuncts.

Professors will teach 4 sections a year, fellows 6, and adjuncts 8 (on a full-time equivalent [FTE] position basis).

Each traditional course will take about 10 hours of work a week. Faculty will generally need to be in class for 4 hours a week. Since the courses are commonly designed, class preparation should take about 4 hours a week and course management about 2. Teaching 3 courses a semester will mean a fellow devotes about 30 hours a week to formal courses. This will leave 5 hours for informal interaction with students and 5 hours for keeping up-to-date in their fields. Thus, the fellow's overall commitment to CELS will be 40 hours a week during the academic year. Fellows will then be free to devote as much time as they wish to professional activities or personal research outside of CELS.

Professors will teach fewer sections. This will give them an additional 10 hours a week to devote to representing CELS to the academic, professional, and local communities and to being CELS thought leaders for their areas.

The columns labeled "Professors," "Fellows," and "Adjuncts" represent the number of faculty needed to teach the necessary sections. Adjuncts will be reported on an FTE basis (e.g., 125 adjuncts represent one class taught by an adjunct). Given our value proposition, the use of adjuncts will be low.[10]

The next columns (Professor, Fellow, and Adjunct Compensation) show the salary and benefit costs for professors, fellows, and adjuncts.[11] Salary costs will vary a great deal by area of concentration. Generally, salary costs will be comparable to those at smaller doctoral-granting universities.[12] These salaries will be competitive with those paid at top liberal arts colleges and research universities, except no premium will be paid to research "stars."

Salaries for fellows will be similar to assistant/associate professor salaries except in high salary areas, particularly business. Here it will be hard to find faculty with a Ph.D. who also have significant real-world experience. Since CELS will require faculty with real-world knowledge and experience, recruiting for these positions will often not compete with research schools. Fellows in these areas will be paid substantially less than what they could earn in business. Pay will be set high enough, however, to be attractive to those who are drawn to the faculty for nonfinancial motives (e.g., they enjoy teaching, being around college students, satisfying their intellectual curiosity, job flexibility and variety, and/or a more relaxed lifestyle[13]).

The total compensation column is the number of faculty by rank multiplied by compensation by rank. The row for core faculty reflects the cost of teaching required core courses. There will not be a separate core faculty, however; these faculty lines will actually be spread among the different areas as appropriate.

The buffer row refers to additional faculty that may be necessary for two reasons: First, actual course enrollment patterns will vary somewhat from the smooth patterns used in these projections. This should not be a major problem, as large class size will be capped at 100 in these projections, while actual course size can go to 125; and small class size will be capped at 5, while actual size can go to 6. The second reason for including a "buffer" in these projections is that the CELS value proposition will include scheduling so that any student can take any course if he or she plans ahead.

The projections by academic area assume offering only one section of a course in a year, unless the projected enrollment exceeds the enrollment cap. To allow students full scheduling options, however, some courses may need to be taught in multiple sections, even though total enrollment will not exceed the cap. Buffer sections will most likely be for courses in one concentration that are also attractive as an elective to students in other concentrations (e.g., Marketing, Communications Performance I, Film I and II, Counseling Skills, etc.).

**Lab Faculty**

| **Labs** | **Students** | **Comp.** | **Fellows** | **Comp.** | **Cost ($000)** |
|---|---|---|---|---|---|
| Communications | — | — | 8 | 55 | 440 |
| Math/Statistics | 2 | 9 | 1 | 60 | 78 |
| Science/Engineering | 2 | 9 | 1 | 60 | 78 |
| Fine Arts | 1 | 9 | 1 | 50 | 59 |
| Senior Tutors | — | — | 1.6 | 72 | 115 |
| Junior Tutors | 30 | 0 | — | — | 0 |
| Other | 2 | 9 | 13 | — | 18 |
| **Total** | — | — | — | — | 788 |

Teaching fellows in the Communications Lab will be responsible for: 1) providing individual evaluation, feedback, and coaching to all students in the required communications course, 2) individual evaluation, feedback, and coaching to all students on the mandatory communications elements integrated into their other core courses, and 3) ad hoc general communications consulting as requested by students. The projections assume one consultant for every 100 first-year students.

One teaching fellow will be responsible for running a lab that provides support in courses in math, statistics, and other quantitative methods (e.g., Thinking Skills, Research Methods in Behavioral Science).

There will be one senior tutor for every house of 200 students. Senior tutors will devote 10% of their time to teaching the personal development courses in their houses. So 1.6 FTE of senior tutors will be charged to instructional expense.

Junior tutors will not be compensated for their role in the first-year personal development courses offered in each house. By graduation, about half of all CELS students will have served one semester as a junior tutor.

In addition to faculty, well-trained and supervised upper-division students will be involved in instruction. Students will also assist in science and engineering labs, the math/statistics lab, and various small labs (e.g., accounting). The number of students shown is an FTE number.

| Other Instructional Expenses | |
|---|---|
| Expense | Cost ($000) |
| Faculty Miscellaneous Operating Expenses (MOE) | 80 |
| Engineering and Science Equipment/Supplies | 100 |
| Copying | 32 |
| **Total** | **212** |

Faculty MOE will be $1,000 per faculty member ($400 for computer, $250 for phone, $100 for general supplies, and $250 for furniture). Copying costs will be $10 per student to copy course handouts.

| Information Technology (IT) | |
|---|---|
| Expense | Cost ($000) |
| IT Software | 16 |
| Central IT Allocated | 196 |
| **Total** | **212** |

IT software will be $5 per student for a course-management system like Blackboard, WebCT, or Desire2Learn.[14] Central IT allocated represents central IT costs allocated to instruction (see schedule).

*Depreciation.* Depreciation is straight-line with a 50-year life. Depreciation is allocated to instruction based on building use (see schedule).

*Physical Plan Operations and Maintenance.* Physical Plan operations and maintenance (PPOM) are allocated to instruction based on the square feet of space used in instruction (see schedule).

## Research and Public Service

In addition to instruction, the other two primary activities of college are research and public service. CELS will do both on a very limited basis, and only as a byproduct of instruction. As a result, all faculty time related to research and public service will be charged to instruction.[15] Thus, CELS will not have any research and public service expenses.

## Academic Support

| Expense | Cost ($000) |
|---|---|
| IT | 1,332 |
| Educational Media | 175 |
| Library | 287 |
| Off-Campus Programs | 122 |
| Senior Tutors | 173 |
| Academic Administration | 583 |
| Faculty Development | 320 |
| Course Development | 480 |
| Depreciation | 84 |
| PPOM | 148 |
| **Total** | **3,703** |

| | IT | | |
|---|---|---|---|
| Expense | Number of Students | Cost per Student | Cost ($000) |
| Hardware | 3,200 | 0.325 | 1,040 |
| Software | 3,200 | 0.030 | 96 |
| Central IT Allocated | — | — | 196 |
| **Total** | — | — | **1,332** |

CELS will provide every student with a laptop. Computer costs per student are estimated, given a useful life of four years (the student keeps the laptop upon graduation). Cost per machine, including four-year warranty, will be $1,300. Software includes Microsoft Office products for all students and software such as AutoCAD or SAS for specialty academic labs.

| | Library[16] | | |
|---|---|---|---|
| Expense | Full-Time Equivalent Position | Compensation per Position | Cost ($000) |
| Director | 0.5 | 72 | 36 |
| Coordinator | 2.0 | 40 | 80 |
| Desk Help | 4.0 | 9 | 36 |
| MOE | — | — | 10 |
| Books/Data | — | — | 125 |
| **Total** | — | — | **287** |

Research will not be a CELS function, so CELS's information needs will be much less than those of a research school. The purpose of the library will be to support CELS's teaching. Field project courses will often be information intensive, while normal courses will require little, if any, information beyond what is available in course texts.

Since CELS will not be a research school and will not maintain large holdings of never-referenced materials (e.g., back issues of print journals), staffing needs will be minor compared to most college libraries. CELS will maintain base holdings of 20,000 books and full access to all relevant electronic databases (e.g., LexisNexis, Academic Source Premier, Business Source Premier, etc.). The annual acquisition budget includes $60,000 for databases, $60,000 for books, and $5,000 for browsing materials (e.g., current issues of newspapers and magazines).

| Expense | Educational Media | | |
|---|---|---|---|
| | Full-Time Equivalent Position | Compensation per Position | Cost ($000) |
| Director | 0.5 | 72 | 36 |
| Senior Technician | 1.0 | 50 | 50 |
| Technician | 2.0 | 20 | 40 |
| Secretary | 1.0 | 24 | 24 |
| Equipment | — | — | 20 |
| MOE | — | — | 5 |
| **Total** | — | — | **175** |

Educational media will provide the technical support necessary to create, package, and deliver course media internally to CELS students.

| Expense | Off-Campus Programs | | |
|---|---|---|---|
| | Full-Time Equivalent Position | Compensation per Position | Cost ($000) |
| Manager | 0.5 | 72 | 36 |
| Coordinator | 1.0 | 40 | 40 |
| Secretary | 1.0 | 24 | 24 |
| Travel | — | — | 15 |
| MOE | — | — | 7 |
| **Total** | — | — | **122** |

Student participation in off-campus programming, both international and domestic, will be encouraged. This office will identify quality programming and manage the interface between specific programs and CELS students.[17]

| | Academic Advising | | |
|---|---|---|---|
| Expense | Full-Time Equivalent Position | Compensation per Position | Cost ($000) |
| Senior Tutors | 2.4 | 72 | 173 |

Fifteen percent of senior tutors' time will be devoted to academic advising for first- and second-year students in their houses. After that, academic advising will be performed by faculty through area of concentration tutorials, and will be charged to instruction.

| | Academic Administration | | |
|---|---|---|---|
| Expense | Full-Time Equivalent Position | Compensation per Position | Cost ($000) |
| Academic Area Coordinator | 7 | 28 | 196 |
| Analyst | 1 | 72 | 72 |
| Administrative Assistant | 4 | 35 | 140 |
| Secretary | 4 | 24 | 96 |
| Student | 2 | 12 | 24 |
| MOE | — | — | 20 |
| Faculty Recruiting | — | — | 35 |
| Total | — | — | 583 |

Academic administration will include the middle tier of academic management. The top tier will be the provost and will be charged to institutional support. The bottom tier will consist of department heads and will be charged to instruction. The middle tier will include the various deans and their offices. At large research universities, the middle tier plays a major role and is expensive to operate. Given CELS's limited size and scope, middle-tier management will be unnecessary. The area coordinator's job will be a mix between a dean and a department head.

There will be one academic coordinator for each area of concentration. In addition to their regular 10-month faculty salary, academic area coordinators will be paid during the summer as compensation for having served as coordinator.

Administrative assistants and secretaries will support the area coordinators and faculty in their areas.[18]

***Faculty development.*** Faculty development will primarily cover attendance at academic and professional meetings, as well as modest out-of-pocket research expenses. It is budgeted at $4,000 annually per faculty member.

***Course development.*** Once designed, all 120 courses will operate in a continuous improvement mode. Annual per-course costs are estimated at $4,000. Compared to other colleges, this is a very large expenditure, but quality course design will be fundamental at CELS.

## Student Services

| Expense | Cost ($000) |
| --- | --- |
| Pastoral Care | 203 |
| Career Services | 277 |
| Student Organizations and Cultural Groups | 984 |
| Recreation/Intramurals | 316 |
| Intercollegiate Athletics | 1,700 |
| Financial Aid | 236 |
| Records | 166 |
| Admissions | 618 |
| Depreciation | 1,303 |
| PPOM | 1,124 |
| IT | 131 |
| Total | 7,057 |

| | Pastoral Care | | |
| --- | --- | --- | --- |
| Expense | Full-Time Equivalent Position | Compensation per Position | Cost ($000) |
| Senior Tutors | 2.4 | 72 | 173 |
| Consulting/Training | — | — | 20 |
| MOE | — | — | 10 |
| Total | — | — | 203 |

"Pastoral care" is a British term for providing students with assistance and guidance in nonacademic issues. Senior tutors will be primarily responsible for pastoral care. They will devote 15% of their time to advising the student-run house government and providing ad hoc, one-on-one assistance to students on a variety of social, emotional, physical, behavioral, moral, and spiritual issues.[19] Sectarian religious activities will be voluntary and will be staffed and financed by outside religious organizations. CELS will not provide mental health or medical services, but will instead refer the student to appropriate service providers in the community.

## Appendix II

| Expense | Career Services | | |
|---|---|---|---|
| | Full-Time Equivalent Position | Compensation per Position | Cost ($000) |
| Director | 1 | 72 | 72 |
| Coordinator | 3 | 40 | 120 |
| Secretary | 1 | 20 | 20 |
| MOE | — | — | 65 |
| **Total** | — | — | **277** |

Career services will be responsible for placing students in jobs upon graduation. CELS's staffing level will be at the high end of existing practice, and its high-quality career services will provide major benefits at a low cost per student.

| Expense | Student Organizations & Cultural Groups | | |
|---|---|---|---|
| | Full-Time Equivalent Position | Compensation per Position | Cost ($000) |
| Program Manager | 2 | 72 | 144 |
| Program Staff | 2 | 40 | 80 |
| Secretary | 1 | 20 | 20 |
| Performing Arts Director | 1 | 72 | 72 |
| Performing Arts Technicians | 1 | 30 | 30 |
| Guest Speakers | — | — | 100 |
| Guest Artists | — | — | 100 |
| Graduation | — | — | 20 |
| Service & Operations | — | — | 30 |
| MOE | — | — | 50 |
| Student Publications Director | 0.25 | 72 | 18 |
| Student Publications Printing | — | — | 30 |
| Student Organizations | — | — | 320 |
| **Total** | — | — | **1,014** |

Students will run student organizations and cultural activities with the program managers and staff coordinating and providing support. Organizational support will be $100 annually to be allocated by students to various student organizations.

Individual speaker fees vary widely. Many business and political speakers do not charge, whereas "professional" speakers can run anywhere from $15,000 to over $100,000.

Students will also primarily run the performing arts portion of social and cultural activities. Programming will be designed to maximize student participation.

The amounts budgeted for guest speakers and artists will be enough to provide an adequate level of quality programming to meet student needs. If the audience is enlarged to include the general community, both programs might be significantly expanded with external ticket sales and sponsorships.

| | Recreation/Intramurals | | |
|---|---|---|---|
| Expense | Full-Time Equivalent Position | Compensation per Position | Cost ($000) |
| Director | 1 | 72 | 72 |
| Coordinator | 3 | 50 | 150 |
| Students | 6 | 9 | 54 |
| MOE | — | — | 40 |
| **Total** | — | — | **316** |

Recreational sports/intramural activities will be popular at CELS. Luckily, most activities either will require no supervision (e.g., jogging, weights, pick-up basketball) or be largely student-run. However, there will a significant gym that will need to stay open 100 hours a week.

**Intercollegiate athletics.** Intercollegiate athletic teams will be NCAA Division III, in which "top" liberal arts schools participate. On the one hand, this will be a huge advantage from a cost standpoint because Division III does not allow athletic scholarships. On the other hand, it will also produce little income from ticket sales and media. CELS will have a high-quality program with football, but not ice hockey (the two most expensive sports). Costs are based on spending at similar schools.[20] The bulk of the cost will go to salaries for coaches and administration.[21]

| | Records | | |
|---|---|---|---|
| Expense | Full-Time Equivalent Position | Compensation per Position | Cost ($000) |
| Registrar | 0.5 | 72 | 36 |
| Coordinator | 1 | 40 | 40 |
| Clerks | 2 | 24 | 48 |
| Secretary | 1 | 24 | 24 |
| Students | 2 | 9 | 18 |
| **Total** | — | — | **166** |

Records will be responsible for class scheduling, course enrollment, and maintenance of student academic records.

| Expense | Financial Aid | | |
|---|---|---|---|
| | Full-Time Equivalent Position | Compensation per Position | Cost ($000) |
| Manager | 1 | 60 | 60 |
| Counselor | 4 | 32 | 128 |
| Clerk | 2 | 24 | 48 |
| **Total** | — | — | **236** |

Financial aid will be responsible for administering institutionally based aid programs and assisting students in locating aid from external sources. Both records and financial aid will be done using existing industry practices and costs.[22]

| Expense | Admissions | | |
|---|---|---|---|
| | Full-Time Equivalent Position | Compensation per Position | Cost ($000) |
| Director | 1 | 130 | 130 |
| Assistant Director | 1 | 75 | 75 |
| Counselors | 4 | 40 | 160 |
| Secretary | 1 | 24 | 24 |
| Students | 3 | 9 | 27 |
| Records Coordinator | 1 | 40 | 40 |
| Records Clerks | 3 | 24 | 72 |
| Travel | — | — | 35 |
| MOE[23] | — | — | 55 |
| **Total** | — | — | **618** |

Admissions will be responsible for marketing and selling CELS to potential students. Compensation for staff will be at current market price.[24] Given that 800 first-year students enroll, cost per student will be $773. This is higher than the average for public schools ($667), but lower than the average for private schools ($2,187).[25] CELS will have lower costs than private schools for several reasons: 1) it will be an easier sell because it is a much better value to the student,[26] 2) it will target recruiting efforts to the region where it will be located rather than send admission counselors around the county, 3) it will operate with no-haggle pricing,[27] 4) it will not attempt to build its applicant pool beyond the size necessary to fill its entering class with qualified students, and 5) it will not aggressively "shape" a class (e.g., try to enroll at least ten women engineering students).[28]

## Institutional Support

| Expense | Cost ($000) |
|---|---|
| Executive Management | 1,224 |
| General Administration | 313 |
| Communications | 264 |
| Alumni & Development | 233 |
| Fiscal & Business | 820 |
| IT | 166 |
| Depreciation | 36 |
| PPOM | 70 |
| Total | 3,126 |

| Executive Management | | | | | |
|---|---|---|---|---|---|
| Executive Management | President | Chief Academic | Chief Business | Chief External | Chief Student |
| Position | 250 | 160 | 160 | 150 | 110 |
| Executive Assistant | 72 | 40 | 40 | 40 | 40 |
| Secretary | 20 | 0 | 0 | 0 | 0 |
| Travel | 20 | 8 | 5 | 20 | 8 |
| Housing/Entertainment | 30 | 0 | 0 | 20 | 5 |
| MOE | 12 | 6 | 2 | 4 | 2 |
| Total | 404 | 214 | 207 | 234 | 165 |

The number of executive positions and their salaries will be based upon current industry norms for private schools of this size.[29] As with other salary figures in these projections, compensation will include 20% for fringe benefits and assume that the school will be located in an area with an average cost of living. There may be some variance in salary based on cost of living.

| General Administration | |
|---|---|
| Expense | Cost ($000) |
| Audit | 30 |
| Legal Fees | 75 |
| Board Costs | 15 |
| Liability Insurance | 30 |
| Directors & Officers Insurance | 33 |
| Institutional Memberships | 20 |
| Staff Development | 25 |
| Board/CEO Consulting | 50 |
| Mail | 35 |
| Total | 313 |

## Appendix II

| Expense | Communications | | |
|---|---|---|---|
| | Full-Time Equivalent Position | Compensation per Position | Cost ($000) |
| Director | 1 | 72 | 72 |
| Specialist | 1 | 60 | 60 |
| Coordinator | 1 | 40 | 40 |
| Technicians | 1 | 40 | 40 |
| Travel | — | — | 5 |
| MOE[30] | — | — | 57 |
| **Total** | — | — | **264** |

Communications will be primarily responsible for general institutional marketing. The major marketing expenses of CELS will be associated with admissions. Following standard accounting practice, sales and marketing costs of admissions will be reported as a student support expense rather than an institutional support expense.

| Expense | Alumni and Development | | |
|---|---|---|---|
| | Full-Time Equivalent Position | Compensation per Position | Cost ($000) |
| Officer | 2 | 72 | 144 |
| Coordinator | 1 | 40 | 40 |
| Student | 1 | 9 | 9 |
| Travel | — | — | 15 |
| MOE[31] | — | — | 25 |
| **Total** | — | — | **233** |

The alumni and development office will be staffed on the assumptions that CELS will not try to fund operating costs out of donations and will not engage in a major capital campaign. Expenses would be significantly higher if that were not the case. Of course, these expenses should generate contributions substantially in excess of their costs.

| Fiscal and Business | | | |
|---|---|---|---|
| Expense | Full-Time Equivalent Position | Compensation per Position | Cost ($000) |
| Bursar | 1 | 60 | 60 |
| Senior Bursar Clerks | 2 | 40 | 80 |
| Bursar Clerks | 3 | 24 | 72 |
|  |  |  | 212 |
| HR Manager | 1 | 60 | 60 |
| HR Clerk | 3 | 24 | 72 |
|  |  |  | 132 |
| Purchasing Manager | 1 | 50 | 50 |
| Purchasing Clerks | 2 | 24 | 48 |
|  |  |  | 98 |
| Assistant Controller | 1 | 72 | 72 |
| Senior Accounting Clerk | 2 | 40 | 80 |
| Accounts Payable Clerk | 2 | 24 | 48 |
|  |  |  | 200 |
| Senior Financial Analyst | 2 | 72 | 144 |
| Student Analyst | 1 | 9 | 9 |
|  |  |  | 153 |
| MOE | — | — | 25 |
| **Total** | — | — | **820** |

Institutional support will also include most finance and administrative functions. These functions will be provided using existing industry practices and costs.[32]

| IT | |
|---|---|
| Expense | Cost ($000) |
| Central IT Allocated | 131 |
| Software | 35 |
| **Total** | **166** |

Software will be for accounting and student records and will cost $11 per student annually.

# Appendix II

## Schedules

| Physical Campus | | |
|---|---|---|
| Use | Square Feet | Cost ($000) |
| Classroom | 54,660 | 8,582 |
| Laboratories | 10,290 | 2,057 |
| Offices | 37,000 | 5,180 |
| Library | 19,553 | 2,776 |
| Auditorium/Theater | 22,000 | 4,405 |
| Student Lounges/Meeting Rooms | 16,000 | 2,288 |
| Recreation Building | 52,000 | 911 |
| Multipurpose Arena | 80,000 | 20,000 |
| Stadium | — | 15,000 |
| Media Production | 5,000 | 950 |
| Support Facilities | 3,000 | 300 |
| **Total** | **299,503** | **70,650** |

An attractive campus is important to residential college students. CELS will have top-of-the-line facilities. Costs will be controlled by not building excess space.

Rather than cost out specific buildings, most physical space needs were assessed at the college level using guidelines published by the Council of Educational Facility Planners International.[33] After space needs were determined, cost of the building was then estimated using national cost data from RSMeans.[34,35]

Because RSMeans costs are for an average building, they were adjusted upward by 20% to account for high-quality upgrades such as iconic architectural elements and above-grade finishes.[36]

The auditorium/theater will be a 350-seat facility with supporting performance and rehearsal space. The multipurpose arena will be a state-of-the-art facility that seats 3,500 people for basketball and over 4,000 for convocations and concerts. Recent breakthroughs in arena design and sound systems and acoustics make it feasible for one facility to serve both purposes.[37] The arena will also be able to generate significant rental revenue from outside organizations and event promoters.

The stadium will seat 3,000 people and offer major college-level amenities. Cost estimates for both the arena and stadium came from a leading architectural firm.[38]

**Depreciation.** The total value of the campus is divided by 50 years to determine depreciation. Depreciation is then charged out to various functions based upon use. Classrooms, labs, and media production will be charged to instruction; the library will be charged to academic support; student lounges and meeting rooms, the auditorium/theater, the recreation building, the multipurpose arena, and the stadium will be charged to student services; support facilities will be charged to institutional support; and office space will be charged to the various functions based on the number of faculty and staff.

***Campus operations and maintenance.*** Campus operations and maintenance will be estimated on a square-footage basis as follows.

| | |
|---|---|
| Cleaning | $0.58 |
| Repair/Maintenance | 1.28 |
| Utilities | 2.18 |
| Roads/Grounds | 0.28 |
| Security | 0.11 |
| Insurance/Administration | 1.84 |
| **Total** | **$6.27**[39] |

Plant operations and maintenance will be charged out to various activities based on building use.

| | IT[40] | | |
|---|---|---|---|
| **Expense** | **Full-Time Equivalent Position** | **Compensation per Position** | **Cost ($000)** |
| Director | 1 | 72 | 72 |
| Staff | 8 | 60 | 480 |
| Student | 3 | 9 | 27 |
| Consulting | — | — | 39 |
| Hardware | — | — | 35 |
| **Total** | — | — | **653** |

IT will be based around student laptops and controlled wireless access to the college network. Because of the limited geographic area on campus and the use of standardized hardware and software, IT will be able to provide an extremely high level of dependability and instructional functionality. Equipment costs assume $140,000 of central computing equipment with a 4-year life. Cost to the central IT office will be charged out to the various functions based on usage: 30% each to instruction and academic support and 20% each to institutional support and student services.

## NOTES

1. C.A. Trigg, "Improving Quality and Reducing Costs: The Case for Redesign," *Course Corrections: Experts Offer Solutions to the College Credit Crisis.* Lumina Foundation For Education, 2005, www.collegecosts.info/pdfs/solution_papers/Collegecosts_%20Oct2005.pdf.
2. Trigg.
3. L. Michealsen, A. Knight, L.D. Fink, *Team Based Learning.* Stylus Publishing, 2002.
4. R.J. Ohara, *The Collegiate Way*, www.collegiateway.org and M.B. Ryan, *A Collegiate Way of Living*, Yale University Press, 2001.
5. Brant Adams, Robert Emerson, Ed Harris, Karen High, and Rick Wilson provided suggestions for coursework in the areas of concentration.
6. Many schools use 3 hours as their primary course length. Adjusting from 4 to 3 hours would require more courses but would not increase costs since faculty course load would be adjusted proportionally.
7. Interest expenses associated with educational activities are negligible at most public and many private schools. The necessary buildings are paid for by either the state or donors.
8. National Association of College and University Business Officers.
9. Public Schools are under Governmental Accounting Standards Board standards and report these expenses separately, while private schools are under Financial Accounting Standards Board standards and allocate expenses out to other activities.
10. Adjuncts are used more in education, following the standard practice of having student teachers supervised on an adjunct basis by retired school teachers.
11. Benefits are assumed at 20% of salary for all CELS employees.
12. Office of Institutional Research and Information Management, *2006-2007 Faculty Salary Survey by Discipline,* Oklahoma State University.
13. A fellow's yearly commitment to CELS is about 40 hours per week for 35 weeks (one week before the fall semester starts; 15 weeks of class per semester; and 2 weeks at the end of each semester for finals, grading and wrap up). This is only about 60% of the time spent at a professional job that requires 46 50-hour work weeks and about 50% of a job with 46 60-hour work weeks. On top of that, faculty work hours are predictable and required travel is modest.
14. All software costs are based on prices currently paid by Oklahoma State University.
15. This is standard industry accounting practice.

16. In this and other category breakouts, the first column is the position or expense category. The second column is the number of people holding that position. The third column in compensation per person for that position. The final column is total compensation for that position or the amount of the other expense category.
17. CELS might also create some travel programs of its own. Any costs associated with CELS trips would be fully covered by program revenues.
18. Arguably, some of the cost of the area coordinators and their offices should be allocated to instruction rather than academic support. For this paper, these costs are allocated wholly to academic support to simplify the presentation of the financials.
19. R. Best, *Pastoral Care and Personal Social Education,* Continuum, 2000.
20. Data for every college are available through "Equity in Athletics," Department of Education, ope.ed.gov/athletics/. The revenue data at this site are not as informative, since it treats all the costs borne by the college as revenue. Every school is therefore shown as breaking even on intercollegiate athletics.
21. For more detail see above or: D.L. Fulks, *2002-03 NCAA Revenues and Expenses of Division III Intercollegiate Athletics Programs Report,* National Collegiate Athletic Association.
22. Personal correspondence with B. Dixon of Oklahoma State University.
23. Miscellaneous operating expenses include a significant amount of marketing collateral (flyers, view books, etc.) This is also true for the other functions with significant marketing, including communications and alumni and development. Most schools run these groups as three separate areas. That practice is reflected in these pro formas. The better practice, however, would be to manage them jointly; see: R.A. Sevier and E. Sickler, "Is Image Still Everything?" Statmats White Paper # 14.
24. Sales force compensation in higher education is low relative to other industries. CELS will explore alternative approaches to admissions aimed at decreasing the cost per student enrolled.
25. *State of College Admissions 2006,* www.nacadnet.org.
26. This assumes that CELS will pass its lower costs on to its students.
27. The average tuition at private schools is often about 40% of its sticker price. The admissions office is responsible for negotiating price with students by making decisions about the level of "institutional scholarship" (a discount from sticker price) to offer each student.
28. Personal correspondence with R.A. Sevier of Statmats.
29. Personal Correspondence with D. Horner of EFT Associates.
30. "Equity in Athletics"

31. "Equity in Athletics"
32. Personal correspondence with B. Dixon.
33. *Space Planning for Institutions of Higher Education,* The Council for Educational Facility Planners International, 2006.
34. There are significant construction costs differences depending on where CELS is located. RSMeans provides a location factor that can be used to adjust national cost to a specific location. In this case, Dallas was assumed as the location.
35. *RSMeans Square Foot Costs 2008*, Reed Construction Data, Inc.
36. The 20% upward adjustment also includes the cost of campus infrastructure (e.g., roads, utility lines, etc.) and landscaping.
37. The facility will bear little resemblance to the multipurpose arenas built in the 1960s–70s. Many of these are still in use today and are substandard for either purpose.
38. Personal correspondence with S. Smith of Ellerbe Becket.
39. Rates are taken from the *2006 BOMA Experience Exchange Report-Average Metropolitan Rate in Oklahoma.*
40. Personal correspondence with M. Weiser of Oklahoma State University.